Learning, Reading and Writing Strategies for the Motivated Student

By

George J. Kingston

authorHOUSE™

1663 LIBERTY DRIVE, SUITE 200
BLOOMINGTON, INDIANA 47403
(800) 839-8640
WWW.AUTHORHOUSE.COM

First published by AuthorHouse 11/15/05

ISBN: 1-4208-6173-5 (sc)

Printed in the United States of America
Bloomington, Indiana

This book is printed on acid-free paper.

ACKNOWLEDGEMENT

The author thanks his wife, Gail, for her support in producing this book.

Table of Contents

LEARNING SKILLS: GOALS AND OBJECTIVES

Are you challenging your mind to work faster and comprehend more in a shorter period? Challenge your mind by thinking more about key issues in your life, solving problems or comprehending greater information in a shorter time frame. Just as you exercise your body for strength, tone and flexibility, exercise your mind to increase mental capacity, reading comprehension, writing skills and enhance memory. Tests have time limits, jobs require timely completed projects; we all have deadlines. We need to learn faster to meet our time-constrained learning goals. Do you have the desire to excel in school, compete for enjoyable, high-paying jobs, start a successful business or create more time for your interests or hobbies? We compete throughout the world for resources and jobs. How well you succeed during your lifetime will depend on your motivation to learn and reach your desired goals.

The **overall goal of this book** is to provide techniques for you to learn more quickly, read faster, increase reading comprehension, improve writing skills and enhance your memory skills. Improving your learning skills can help you in many of your endeavors such as improving grades or job performance and gaining more time to do other things such as hobbies, sports or even read more enjoyable books. Ask yourself what you want to learn; what are your specific learning goals? Make your goals accountable, defined, measurable, realistic and relevant with a time limit. For example, in a high school history class you are accountable for your work. The teacher defines the material on the test and measures your performance with a grade. The realistic test will take place. The teacher will test you on the relevant material on a specific date with a maximum time limit. Write down your goals and develop a plan to obtain them using the techniques discussed in this book.

CRITICAL SUCCESS FACTORS

What are the critical success factors necessary to improve your learning capabilities, which will help you succeed in your learning endeavors?

➢ Motivated to learn the required information

➢ Use of formal and informal learning

➢ Physical and mental skills or techniques necessary for specific learning goal, job or performance

➢ Optimal learning environment

➢ Use optimal intelligence for learning input

➢ Use critical thinking and reasoning skills

➢ Previous experience, knowledge or skills related to your new learning endeavor

➢ Understand and memorize relationships between key ideas

➢ Do required problems or assignments to comprehend material

➢ Strengthen study habits and testing skills

➢ Use enhanced memory techniques

➢ Use all of your senses to absorb information

➢ Test yourself with generated questions

➢ Schedule review sessions

➢ Rewards you will receive for achieving the final desired outcome (grades, prestige, power, advancement, promotions, disposable income or other)

➢ Reading efficiency enhances learning efficiency

Learning Environment

Prepare your mind before you absorb new information. Your environment helps you learn at a quicker rate. A low-stress, relaxed atmosphere allows your mind to unlock itself and become resourceful. Classical music improves your mood, emotions, alertness and receptiveness. Develop a positive mental attitude toward learning. Enthusiasm and optimism generate positive emotions, which help you learn faster. Doubt, fear, worry and tension reduce your capacity to rapidly learn or think and cause a break in the subconscious learning process. Have you ever taken a test and your mind could not function, known as blanking out, because you reached a panic state from the negative thoughts of failing or not finishing the test? Believe in yourself. Continue to tell yourself that you learn and concentrate easily on the new material, which then enters your subconscious mind. Your subconscious mind obeys your own positive statements to yourself. Tell yourself that you will reach your goal, such as earn top grades, compete at a higher level, improve college opportunities, find better job opportunities, or increase enjoyment or satisfaction.

Relaxation Techniques

Meditation helps you relax into a restful state of mind for efficient absorption of new information. Meditation reduces heart rate, blood pressure, perspiration, tension and respiratory rate and enables the body to establish an optimal balance. Meditation triggers immune cells that fight against bacterial infections, viruses and other ailments, including stress. To meditate, close your eyes. Focus your mind continuously on one positive thought, word, sound, phrase, action or prayer. If your mind wanders, concentrate on a specific thought. Eliminate negative thoughts that block your inner positive energy. The more focused and relaxed your mind becomes, the faster information will flow to you. An example of a meditation: Close your eyes and concentrate on the sensation of each deep breath. Another form of mediation is to concentrate on nothing; let your mind completely rest.

Self-hypnosis also helps your mind to absorb information in a relaxed, focused state. Once in the self-induced hypnotic state, your receptivity to suggestions or learning new information coming into your subconscious mind increases. Tape record your suggested new information before your hypnotic session. Start in a comfortable position, close your eyes and concentrate on taking long, deep breaths. Once you feel comfortable, concentrate on tightening and relaxing each muscle in your body. Now, listen to your suggestions or information already recorded on the tape. At a later study session, recall, outline or answer questions related to the information you absorbed from your hypnotic session. Once mentally relaxed through meditation or self-hypnosis in a quiet environment, start applying the various learning techniques discussed in this book.

INFORMAL/FORMAL LEARNING

Do you learn quicker through informal or formal learning?

If you enjoy independence with less structure, then an informal learning environment may improve your learning efficiency. Informal learning consists of cooperative projects, trial and error, conversation, new exploration, play, question-and-answer group sessions, discussions and experiments. Formal learning involves less group involvement, more exercises, lectures, textbooks, and step-by-step procedures as in a classroom atmosphere. Some of us require more structure and others more independence when we learn.

INTELLIGENCE

We have a dominant form of intelligence that helps us learn new material. We need to understand what type of intelligence helps us learn more quickly with greater comprehension and understanding. How will understanding your intelligence type help your learning efficiency?

Intelligence represents the capacity to learn, reason, understand, critically think, grasp facts, understand relationships, solve problems, use logic or any other form of mental activity. Our ability to act and react in an ever-changing environment represents intelligence.

The speed at which we comprehend, absorb, examine and respond to new information measures intelligence. Your specific actions to obtain your goal or goals represent intelligence. Your learning capacity also improves as you use your intelligence to absorb and retain information. Some of us do better in math than English; others are better athletes, painters, musicians, designers or language specialists. Your dominant intelligence allows you to learn and comprehend faster by inputting the information in a format relating to that intelligence. Let's examine some of the different types of intelligence. Once you understand your dominant intelligence, then develop strategies to improve your learning efficiency.

Linguistic intelligence involves a person's strong ability to construct, apply and comprehend language. Use reading, speaking and writing skills to learn. Write and/or tape record your notes. Discuss the study material with others.

Mathematical intelligence involves logical explanations, numbers, problem solving, flow charts, diagrams, patterns or step-by-step processes. This person rapidly processes logical problems and equations. Put study notes in a logical form just like solving a math problem. Draw flow charts, diagrams and create patterns.

Visual, or spatial intelligence, located in the right hemisphere of your brain, involves sight, three-dimensional images, pictures, mental images, underlining, films, slides, video, tapes, compact disks or any other visual media. Create images, graphs, illustrations, charts, pictures and other visual study aids to help you learn.

Musical intelligence involves rhythms, natural sounds, songs, poems, jingles or an aptitude toward musical instruments. Scientifically pinpointed areas of the brain affect the ability to perform and compose music. Put new information in a musical format such as poems, jingles, songs or rhythmic patterns.

Physical intelligence involves physical activities, role-playing, modeling, games, touching, acting and kinesthesia—the sense of weight, position and movement. Each person possesses a certain control of his or her movements, balance, agility and grace. This individual senses how their body should act and react in a demanding physical situation. Each hemisphere of the brain controls the opposite side of the body's movements. Use physical activities to stimulate your learning, such as skits, plays, writing notes or hands-on learning techniques. Rewrite notes in an outline form or on note cards. Underline or highlight key information that appears in your study material.

Interpersonal intelligence involves people with strong social skills, who communicate, interact and understand others well. They influence others, notice distinctions and contrasts in others moods, temperaments, motivations and intentions. Politicians, successful salespeople, teachers, leaders, mediators, negotiators and clergy exhibit high interpersonal skills. Compare notes in study groups, teach your new knowledge to others or create other interactive sessions to learn the new material.

Intrapersonal intelligence involves the cognitive ability of self-awareness, such as reflection on one's thoughts, images, ideas and concepts. They challenge opinions or participate in informal discussions. They recognize their own feelings and manage emotion in situations. Intrapersonal types control fears, anxieties, anger and sadness. They channel emotions to reach their goals. This intelligence creates strong emotional self-control by delaying gratification and stifling negative impulses. They empathize toward others feelings, concerns and perspectives. They appreciate the differences in how people feel about things. Intrapersonal types form an accurate model of themselves to operate effectively in life. Asking who we are, what feelings we have and why we are this way can lead to high self-esteem, self-enhancement and strength of character used to solve internal problems and reach specific learning goals.

Emotional intelligence, a combination of interpersonal and intrapersonal intelligence, measures social skills, interpersonal competence, psychological maturity and emotional awareness. Emotional intelligent types monitor their own and others emotions, discriminate among emotions and therefore help them guide their actions.

Auditory intelligence involves the ability to speak out loud or listen to new information. Read your material aloud to yourself. Tape record your notes and play them back.

The different types of intelligence involve your **senses**. We see things—visual, hear things—auditory, taste things or touch things—physical, creating a total sensory experience. To help you find your dominant intelligence, determine which senses work best for you. The more you use the various senses in your learning experience, the faster you will learn. Your learning capacity improves as you combine various intelligences and senses. Let's learn techniques to use your senses and intelligences together.

Visualization sharpens your senses by focusing on images of a desired outcome or process. Transcend into your meditated or relaxed state and visualize in a step-by-step process until you see the desired result or your specific learning goal.

The more you see, do and hear something, the greater the chances you will efficiently learn the new information. **Writing** allows you to see it, do it and hear it. Writing the new material on index cards and then sorting them in a logical order stimulates the various senses. **Explaining or teaching** the information you just learned to someone else helps you reinforce the new information by seeing, hearing and performing the learning task. Reflect on the new information with others or compare notes to stimulate many of the senses. Arguing for or against a topic you are learning forces you to use your various senses. Use your imagination. Create ways to use as many of your senses as you can to improve your learning efficiency and experience.

Do you have a strong curiosity to learn new information? Start by **asking questions**. Open-ended questions involve asking who, what, how, when and why. Are you asking the right questions? This will help you increase your problem-solving skills and attain your desired learning objective. Are you looking at the topic from a different perspective? What are the various points of view? Keep an open mind and search for multiple answers to help solve problems more efficiently. Differentiate between facts and opinions. Find the key points, facts or themes. Predict the questions for your next test. After your last review of the material, try to answer your questions just as you will do on the test. Correct your answers and learn from your mistakes. Question your own beliefs and assumptions. How has the learning experience changed your attitude, perception or belief? Generate appropriate questions and your learning efficiency increases.

Explore available **resources** to improve your learning experience. Encyclopedias, government documents, interviews, maps, almanacs, autobiographers, dictionaries, observations, media, books, Internet, TV, radio, newspaper, magazines, experts, family, teachers, photographs, textbooks, religious leaders, bosses, friends, associates, successful people, mentors and your own experiences are available. Use reliable and valid resources to enhance your learning experience.

Create an **intelligence diagram (ID)**. The diagram will help you organize ideas, outline key words, and create impressions or images through graphic expression of your thoughts. The main topic, subject or theme starts in the center of page. Connect key words with lines to the central topic. Find associations among key words. Absurd and unusual associations stimulate your memory. Focus on the most appropriate key word. On each line, use color, pictures and symbols to illustrate relationships. Look for combinations, connections, analogies or similes. A simile, a figure of speech, describes, explains or compares something between two different objects or ideas by using a connective word such as **like** or **as**. For example, **He is as strong as an ox** or **she ran like a deer.** When you drop the connecting word **like**, the simile becomes a metaphor. A metaphor, a figure of speech, expresses an idea taken from one field of experience to something in another field. Repeated common words of a metaphor stimulate your senses. A **table leg**, **the Lord is my shepherd** or **all the world is a stage** represent metaphors. A mixed metaphor uses two or more unrelated metaphors in the same expression, such as **take the high road, keep the powder dry, I smell a rat** or **we shall nip it in the bud**. Use figures of speech to help you see relationships and patterns. Antonyms (words that have opposite meanings) or synonyms (words that have similar meanings) represent analogies. For example, **fish** is to **swim** as **bird** is to **fly**. Embrace uncertainty, ambiguity or paradox to stimulate your mind. Use opposites for dramatic emphasis. Humor, riddles and puzzles also stimulate the mind to learn new concepts. Develop your intelligence diagram with your imagination and have fun with your new learning technique. Once you have finished, memorize your intelligence diagram; then recreate it on a blank sheet of paper. This exercise will improve your memory skills and understanding of the material.

INTELLIGENCE DIAGRAM

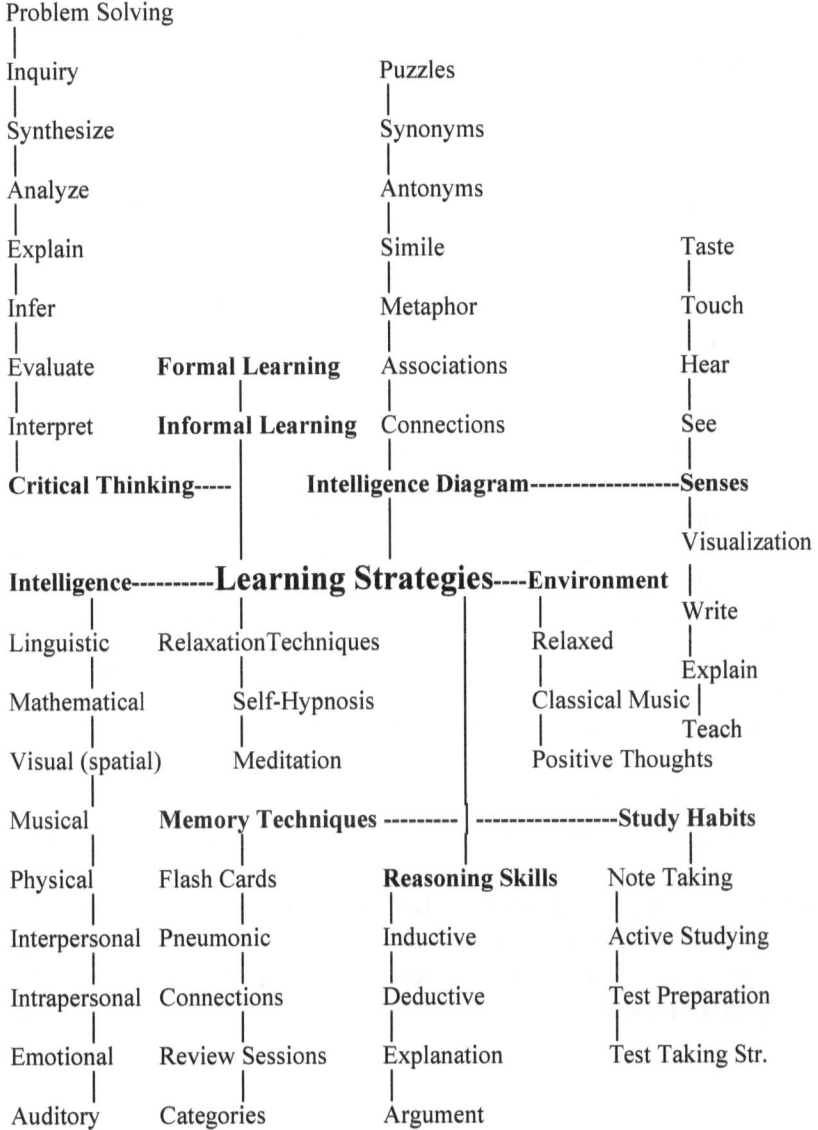

Problem Solving
|
Inquiry   Puzzles
| |
Synthesize   Synonyms
| |
Analyze   Antonyms
| |
Explain   Simile   Taste
| | |
Infer   Metaphor   Touch
| | |
Evaluate   **Formal Learning**   Associations   Hear
| | |
Interpret   **Informal Learning**   Connections   See
| | | |
Critical Thinking-----   **Intelligence Diagram------------------Senses**
                        | | |
                        | | Visualization
                        | | |
Intelligence----------Learning Strategies----Environment |
        | | | Write
Linguistic   RelaxationTechniques   Relaxed |
        | | | Explain
Mathematical   Self-Hypnosis   Classical Music |
        | | | Teach
Visual (spatial) Meditation   Positive Thoughts
        |
Musical   **Memory Techniques ---------| ------------------Study Habits**
        | | | |
Physical   Flash Cards   **Reasoning Skills**   Note Taking
        | | | |
Interpersonal Pneumonic   Inductive   Active Studying
        | | | |
Intrapersonal Connections   Deductive   Test Preparation
        | | | |
Emotional   Review Sessions   Explanation   Test Taking Str.
        | | |
Auditory   Categories   Argument

Memory Techniques

Learn facts, statistics, outlines or summaries with various memory techniques. Use flashcards by writing a question on one side and the answer on the other side. Summarize and categorize your flashcards. Use a pneumonic memory technique by representing the first letter of each word. For example, IRS stands for Internal Revenue Service. NATO stands for North American Treaty Organization. Create an intelligence diagram and then recreate it. Drive the new information from short-term memory to long-term memory by using positive emotion and enthusiasm. How do you access the information when you need it? Taking notes allows you to see, hear and act on the information. Using a combination of your senses will help you memorize the learned information. Form associations, categories and groups of the old knowledge with the new. Connect ideas or images. Turn abstract ideas into specific or concrete ideas. Remember unusual funny facts and contradictions. Match emotions with words or subjects. Use humor, strange ideas, colors and details. Look for words and phrases with strong meaning. What are the key points? You recall more at the beginning and end of a session; therefore, take regular breaks. Divide your study session into smaller sessions. Schedule reviews for the newly learned information. Reorganize information with an outline or intelligence diagram. Outline subject, major headings, subheadings and key words. Look for strong connections between data, ideas, concepts or principles. Summarize the material outlined or paraphrase the information. Organize your thoughts with index cards. Break down the material into small steps. Create a mental picture of the information. Recreate your outline, intelligence diagram or study notes from memory. Create questions from your notes. Concentrate full attention on your learning goal. Complete one goal at a time using these memory techniques.

Learning Behavior

How does new information relate to what you already know? Use comparisons, associations or other mental or physical techniques to integrate previously learned and new information. Review from previous sessions. Show or demonstrate what you learned. Practice until the behavior becomes a habit. Does your specific behavior help you attain your learning goal? If not, then change that behavior. Use self-discipline to improve your learning skills by changing your behavior. Give yourself a reward for each step accomplished toward your goal. Reward yourself immediately or at least intermittently to continue the positive behavior. Use deferred rewards in conjunction with immediate or intermittent rewards. The more you receive positive feedback for your behavior, the more you will continue to follow that behavior. Society, bosses, parents and the law provide feedback (appreciation, money, recognition, awards from peers, vacations) for your behavior. Repeat your acquired learning behaviors to obtain your intended learning goals. Create a study schedule in a quiet atmosphere and stay with your plan to learn.

Reasoning Skills

Reasoning skills require you to base your decision on reliable facts, evidence or logical conclusions. Consider various options before you make a decision. Rely on the evidence and common sense to make sound decisions. Do not let emotions overpower or cloud your thoughts of logic and reason that support your decisions or actions.

Inductive reasoning draws inferences or conclusions from specific facts, data, observations or evidence to support a generalization or claim. A large sample of relevant observations creates stronger evidence (premises) to support the conclusion or generalization. Does the conclusion follow logically from the premise or premises? Do not stereotype by making generalizations or conclusions about an entire group from observations of a small segment of that group. Biased observations, sources, data or evidence form biased generalized conclusions.

Analogies represent one form of inductive reasoning. An analogy represents a logical relationship to define new terms, explain processes, illustrate your point or compare and show similarities. If two or more things are similar in some respects, then one could conclude that they are probably similar in some other respect. Take information already known and find similarities with the new information. To determine the analogy, find that relationship (characteristic, degree, function, purpose). Use antonyms and synonyms to form an analogy. If an item represents a subset of a category in which one word names something that falls into the group, then the second relationship would follow a similar relationship pattern. For example, **beagle** is to **dog** as **robin** is to **bird**. The number of instances, their relevance and number of similarities affect the strength of inductive inference. The more examples and data used in the inductive reasoning process, the greater the validity of the generalization.

Cause and effect represents another form of inductive reasoning. Does the particular action or actions cause the result or effect? Consider other causes that could create the effect. Observe what occurred differently from the normal pattern and what occurred consistently over time (common variable). Did an additional factor affect the common variable? Do not assume that because *X* happens before *Y*, a logical connection occurred between *X* and *Y*. An effect may have many causes. Evaluate the evidence and use the process of elimination to form a valid conclusion.

Use **statistics** as evidence to help validate a conclusion. Evaluate the statistic by considering the source. Unbiased expertise improves the credibility of the source. Use representative, random and large sample sizes to generate accurate figures that reflect the data and source. Make sure statistics compare similar items.

Deductive reasoning starts with a general major premise or conclusion and creates a minor premise or evidence that logically follows the major premise to form a valid, specific conclusion. Many major premises are untrue or implied; therefore, the conclusion becomes untrue. For example, all birds eat worms; a blue jay is a bird; therefore, all blue jays eat worms. The major premise may not be true. All birds do not eat worms, creating a false conclusion. Avoid all-inclusive expressions such as **everyone** or **all**. One can usually find an exception. Show how each statement logically relates to each other. If event *A* occurs before event *B*, do not assume event *A* caused event *B*. Do not reach a conclusion with biased or unreliable sources. Use facts, not opinions, for your evidence in your premises and conclusions. If you rely on expert testimony, make sure their expertise relates to your particular subject. A logical, valid conclusion shows concrete examples without violating the reader's common sense with unreasonable statements in the major or minor premise when using deductive reasoning.

Identify the conclusion, main claim, point of view or argument when reading or writing new material. Conclusions may have many premises. A premise may independently support the conclusion. Other premises work together to support the conclusion. Differentiate a minor conclusion from each dependent premise and the main or overall conclusion. Words indicating a conclusion: **accordingly, as a result, consequently, hence, it follows that, means, shows, so, suggests that, that's why** and **thus.** Words indicating a premise: **as indicated by, as shown by, because, for, given, inasmuch as, since, that,** and **the reason is that**. The conclusion may appear before or after any premise. What does the author (yourself) ultimately communicate to the reader (convince you, change belief, ask for action)?

Examine each premise (evidence) for credibility and reason. If premises lack validity, the reader will disagree with the author's conclusion, main claim, point of view or argument. Does the author have credibility? Are the sources providing credible, unbiased evidence (premise) and expertise in the specific field related to the subject? Determine expertise by education, experience, job, reputation and achievements. Determine if a premise represents beliefs, experiences, expert testimony, facts, figures, observations, opinions, physical evidence, statistics, tentative truths (unverifiable truths) or witness testimony. A reasonable, clear premise represents credible evidence in a logical order supporting your conclusion. Major premises support the conclusion and minor premises (details) support each major premise. Raise a red flag for a premise stating **all** or **none** because of the strong exception possibility. Do euphemisms, dysphemisms or biased questions replace credible and reasonable evidence? Does the conclusion lack credible premises? Provide other possible views for your focused topic. Use credible and clear major and minor premises to counter opposing premises and conclusions.

Some writers attempt to convince the reader by appealing to emotions (fear, flattery, pressure and pity) rather than logic and reason. The author or speaker attempts to frighten the reader to act without logical reasoning based on credible evidence, which leads to poor decisions. The author attempts to flatter the reader and then asks for action or a response, which may cause a poor decision. Peer pressure may also create a poor decision without a logical basis. The group may not make the best decision; why should you follow the wrong path? An author may appeal to your sense of pity and compassion for others, but this technique may not have merit. Do not fall into the trap of thinking that there are only two possibilities for a solution to a problem. Consider other solutions to the problem. Use your reasoning skills to review the situation and decide on the optimal decision or action. Do not fall into the cause-and-effect trap. If Y happens, then Z will follow. Do not assume this is a causal relationship. Question an author who states the conclusion, then restates the conclusion in a premise or as evidence and does not provide proof of the original conclusion. Question an author who, instead of analyzing the claim or problem, attacks the person's personality, actions, beliefs, affiliations, nationality, ethnicity, appearance, occupation or other categorization rather than the credibility of the major and minor premises or conclusion. Sometimes the author attempts to add an unrelated topic to cloud the true issue or turn potential negative attention away from themselves and onto others. What support does the author provide for their conclusion or point of view? Authors may distort, exaggerate, misrepresent or oversimplify an opposing party's position and then attack that manipulated position. Focus on the specific, valid and credible, major or minor premises and a reasonable, logical conclusion.

An **argument** attempts to convince you that a conclusion is true. An **explanation** attempts to convince you with a true and valid conclusion. Does the explanation show relevance to the subject matter? Can you verify the explanation with a particular methodology? When using deductive or inductive reasoning, does the writer provide strong evidence that creates a credible and reasonable conclusion? Specific and relevant evidence increases the strength of the conclusion. Rely on true facts (evidence) and not emotional details representing opinions to form your conclusion in the explanation.

CRITICAL THINKING

Critical thinking awakens your mind to comprehend, understand and memorize new material. Critical thinking consists of various approaches to problem solving, achieving learning objectives, discussing the issues, considering a situation and making responsible, creative or original decisions. Critical thinking requires strong, inquisitive, open-minded, flexible, creative and persistent behavior to reach your intended objective. Given a specific learning objective within a critical thinking framework, you interpret, evaluate, infer, explain, analyze, synthesize, judge or inquire to produce the desired result (optimal solution).

To **interpret** information, review the data, facts, criteria, rules and experiences. Clarify meaning of key words, charts or graphs. Separate the main ideas from subordinate ideas. Paraphrase research in your own words. Identify the author's purpose, theme, point of view and state any question with precision. Other types of interpretation require recall, recognition, classification, sequencing, visualization, hypothesizing, predicting or drawing conclusions.

To **evaluate** information, state your opinion, judge or take a position on a specific topic. Your conclusion will result from your own criteria, value system or standard. Experiences, data or other information relevant to your subject will impact your evaluation of the material under investigation. What standards or significant factors help express your opinion or judgment of the subject?

To **infer** information, identify or draw reasonable conclusions from relevant information, principles, evidence, data, beliefs, opinions or experiences. Predict the consequences from conjecture or hypothesis of the subject. Confirm or disconfirm a hypothesis. Clarify the meaning of your information and synthesize new ideas or solutions from your present sources.

Explain the information through concepts, theories, principles or evidence. Why did you come to a specific answer or judgment? State your finding through your logical (inductive or deductive) reasoning or procedures. What methods, criteria, evidence, sources or context did you use to make your decision? Present arguments for or against your view. Construct visual diagrams or charts to convey your findings.

Analyze the information by identifying the relationships among statements, questions, concepts or descriptions. Examine the ideas, beliefs, judgments, reasons, information or opinions. Are any arguments for or against the issue under discussion? Identify all assumptions, either stated or unstated. Find the main conclusion. Explain the reasons to support or oppose the stated conclusion. Determine the main purpose of the reading material. How does each sentence and paragraph relate to each other? Compare the strengths and weaknesses of the conclusion. Determine the credibility of the information or sources. Does the evidence or do the premises support the conclusion? Separate and examine the information and show how the parts relate to the whole. After your analysis of the information, can you develop any new perspectives, insights or novel approaches to the subject matter?

To **synthesize** information, take the results from your evaluation, interpretation, inference or explanations and develop new thoughts, concepts, ideas, techniques or processes.

Critical thinking opens your mind to developing your own methods for learning new material. You will become well informed, have a clear understanding of the issues, make reasonable inquiries, improve self-confidence in learning and develop your own form of self-regulated learning. Monitor your own critical thinking by examining the methods used to learn the subject material. Does any personal bias or self-interest influence your thinking process? Do you separate personal opinions and assumptions from other sources such as the author's message? Analyze the factors used in finalizing a conclusion. Review your critical thinking methods (interpret, evaluate, infer, explain, analyze and synthesize) and then revise your statements or conclusions. This review cements what you learned and creates a feeling of high confidence in yourself that you understood the material without any major flaws.

Conduct an Inquiry

Observe, question and form a **hypothesis**, an educated guess or explanation about why or how something happened based on observations. Test the hypothesis by conducting an investigation. Design an experiment by choosing your experimental and control variables. Record your observations and any measurable data. Consider possible explanations for the results and draw a conclusion. Consider other ways to test the hypothesis. Does the outcome raise other questions?

Problem-Solving Skills

First, identify the problem and break it down into key issues, factors or parts. Second, rank the relevant issues of the problem and then address each issue. Find the key facts and true statements to help you solve the problem. Document your credible sources to verify your facts. The more credible the source, the greater the reader will believe the facts used to justify your answer to the problem. Consider the credibility of a source by the level of expertise and bias. Determine the level of expertise by education, experience, position, reputation and any achievements in the particular field. Determine if the expert source has a bias toward any of your issues or the problem. Do not rely on emotional opinions as facts, which may not represent a true statement. Use relevant facts or evidence to support your opinion, assumptions or point of view. One can debate opinions, but not facts. When reviewing the evidence, determine who generated the information. Researchers may manipulate data, studies, tests or results to give a biased conclusion. Review the denotation and connotation for each word used. Does the author use euphemisms or dysphemisms to convey a particular point of view, manipulate feelings or influence one's thoughts on a particular issue? Biased questions attempt to generate an unfair response. Recognize these subtle persuasive techniques and form your own independent conclusions on the subject. Finally, review the possible logical solutions to the problem and select the optimal solution backed by the unbiased facts generated from your analysis of the problem.

Study Habits

Mastering a new subject requires effort, hard work and perseverance. Make study time a priority. Effective study periods generate knowledge and excellent grades. Time invested in studying leads to mastery of the subject. Slow-learning students have to study longer and harder. Hopefully, after reading and applying the ideas in this book, those study sessions will shorten and improve learning retention. Organize a study area and schedule study time. During study time, reduce all other activities, distractions or interruptions. Generally, one learns more quickly if he or she concentrates on the required material during several shorter study sessions spaced out over several days. Plan a favorite activity after your study session. As you study your information, ask yourself: Do I understand what I've just read? What's the main idea? Have I grasped the key concepts? Plan review sessions before each test.

Note Taking

Define the purpose for taking notes. Write the information necessary for the test, assignment or work. Use some form of shorthand to abbreviate key words. Write down key concepts, principles, topics, ideas and words from the speaker or written material. Write questions in the margins of your notes. Condense, summarize and paraphrase significant ideas from your notes as quickly and neatly as possible. Practice writing down important information the teacher puts on the blackboard. Review new material on your predetermined study schedule. People tend to retain more information and develop greater understanding if they review soon after the initial introduction of material. Rewrite the notes into an organized outline for your study review. Complement your notes with textbook or other assigned readings. Create an intelligence diagram for each topic or assignment. Learn to study with others and follow the rules of good teamwork by concentrating on mastering the required material by a particular date. Trade ideas (notes), divide work, ask questions, and speak respectfully and quietly to others. Develop enough self-discipline to keep the study session from deteriorating into a gab session.

Active Studying

Active studying examines details, assumptions, evidence, illustrations, examples, opinions, conclusions and unique points. Stay alert to the material. Ask yourself questions about the information. Identify main ideas and facts after reading a paragraph or page. Stop and identify the key ideas in that section by generating an intelligence diagram. Write down main concepts, important dates, names and terms. Write a quick summary of what you just read. Use those notes to review the lesson. Outline the text. For example, just after you read one of the classics for your English class, describe the setting, main characters, sequence of action, main conflict, resolution and theme. Create a chart or diagram. Categorize new terms or ideas, develop a timeline and draw a quick picture to represent what you learned. Explain the new information to a parent, friend or yourself. Connect new material with previously learned knowledge. Use examples as much as possible.

Test Preparation

Know the test date and what the test will encompass, such as chapters, handouts, lecture notes or other key information. Will the test have short-answer, essay or multiple-choice questions? Create test questions from your study material in a similar format. Prepare a review schedule and practice on a regular basis. Organizational skills and perseverance produce high test scores. The summaries at the end of each chapter often highlight information or include practice questions for the test review. During classroom reviews, focus on the information the teacher emphasizes, questions they repeat, sections of the book they review or information they write on the board or handout. Take practice tests from the questions you generated from the required material. Spend extra time on trouble spots. Get a good night's sleep before test day. A rested brain allows for clear thinking and recall of the test material. Eat a nourishing breakfast on the morning of the test; your brain and body require energy to perform well mentally and physically.

Test-Taking Strategies

Read the directions carefully. Scan the whole test and allocate time for each section or question. Budget more time to sections or questions on the test that generate more points. Read each question carefully to understand what you are required to answer. Underline key words of the question. If you have a problem with certain questions, return to them after answering the remaining test questions. Don't get bogged down on any one question or problem. On essay questions, briefly outline before you begin to answer the question. Use meditative techniques to reduce test anxiety before or during the test. If you have extra time, double-check your answers, search for mistakes, rework calculations and proofread essay answers.

Monitor Your Children in School

Examine the school curriculum. Communicate with teachers about your child's homework, test scores and class behavior. At home, control TV and Internet usage. Monitor your child's health. Are they receiving enough sleep, eating enough healthy foods and exercising daily? Expect your children to do the best they can. Children respond well to structure. Use a parent or another person to act as a tutor, coach, trainer, cheerleader or referee.

LEARNING SKILLS SUMMARY

➢ Determine your specific, quantitative goal(s) or objective(s).

➢ Review the critical success factors.

➢ Develop a relaxed, stress free learning environment.

➢ Use meditation or self-hypnosis to increase learning.

➢ Use an informal or formal learning structure.

➢ Format information with your dominant intelligence.

➢ Use as many of your senses to absorb information.

➢ Visualize, write, explain, teach, ask questions and use multiple resources for improved learning.

➢ Create an intelligence diagram to organize key ideas.

➢ Use various memory techniques such as flashcards, pneumonic techniques or intelligence diagrams.

➢ Relate previously learned information with new information.

➢ Develop inductive and deductive reasoning skills.

➢ Develop your critical thinking techniques through interpretation, evaluation, inference, explanation, analysis and synthesis.

➢ Conduct an inquiry and experiment.

➢ Improve your problem solving skills.

➢ Improve your study habits, note taking skills and active studying techniques.

➢ Review test preparation and test taking techniques.

➢ Learning a new subject requires perseverance, hard work and motivation. Use your imagination, intuition, vision and creativity to enhance your learning experience.

➢ Eat a proper diet to enhance your memory and brain function for optimal learning.

Reading Techniques

Read to improve your vocabulary, comprehension and speed. Learn new information about many subjects in life, your job, hobbies or interests, through your increased reading skills.

Physical Reading Techniques

Avoid rereading words or sentences. Read between the black lines to reduce eye tension. Use steady, rhythmic eye movements by choosing key words and phrases. Cover at least two or three words on either side of the main word.

Determine your **reading rate** for best comprehension based on your familiarity with the material, the difficulty level, vocabulary, background of knowledge, experience, importance and your purpose. Use a high-speed reading rate for a quick overview or to search for a specific fact or facts. Read faster than normal for easy material, when rereading old material or when searching for main ideas. Read at your normal rate when focusing on main ideas, important details or quality pleasure reading. Read slower than normal when comprehending difficult material such as focusing on details for a test, learning a job skill, critically evaluating projects or interpreting poetry. Read with a purpose: retain or recall information, select important points, interpret information; make general conclusions, judgments or inferences. Relate your reading to previous experiences. Test your comprehension by creating an intelligence diagram. Reflect on what you just read and write down the key points.

To improve your **reading efficiency**, pre-read the material. Most writers organize their material with an introduction, development of the introduction and conclusion. Read the introduction or the first two or three paragraphs thoroughly. Read the first sentence of each remaining paragraph and finally read the conclusion. Notice key words and ideas that are boldfaced, highlighted, bulleted or boxed. Review the summaries, headings and highlighted information. Continue to ask how each idea connects to the major reading topic— the main idea that holds the paragraphs and sentences together.

Look for those factual clues (evidence) that generate the author's message. Highlight or underline key words, unfamiliar words, phrases and ideas. Learn unfamiliar words from the context of the sentence or paragraph. Use a dictionary to learn the word. Does the new word have a particular connotation? Write questions in the margins relating to these words and concepts. Distinguish between major facts, minor facts and opinions. Review your highlighted information by forming an outline to memorize and comprehend. Write answers to your generated questions. Use your notes to form inferences—conclusions generated from your facts, evidence and logical reasoning. Judge the validity of the author's analysis. Are the author's ideas logical? Does the author support conclusions with credible evidence?

Active reading requires focused concentration to evaluate or analyze the author's message. Underline new ideas and concepts from the paragraphs. Try to anticipate what will happen next as you read. Locate the topic sentence in each paragraph. The remaining sentences should support the topic sentence. Read to understand, not just to memorize. Find verifiable facts to support the assumptions, opinions or point of view. Distinguish between major and minor facts and opinions. When reading a passage for a test, look for the facts in the text only. Do not add extra information unmentioned or assumed. Distinguish the logical order throughout the passage such as chronological order, order of importance, compare and contrast or cause and effect. Does the author use the first-person, second-person or third-person point of view to communicate with the reader? Identify unfamiliar vocabulary. Define unfamiliar words using a dictionary or the context of surrounding words. Focus on boldfaced, highlighted, bulleted or boxed key words and ideas. Review summaries, heading and highlighted information. How does each idea connect to the main topic? Highlight or underline key words and phrases. Write questions in the margins relating to the ideas and concepts in each paragraph. Form an outline from your highlighted information. Write answers to your generated questions. Create conclusions from your outline and questions. Record any reactions in the margins. Notice the writer's particular use of words and phrases—their diction—that can reveal how the author feels about the subject. Acknowledging an author's style improves the understanding of the ideas and message. Underline key facts and details about people, places and things. Make valid inferences, conclusions based on reason, fact or evidence, from your observations.

Comprehension includes the purpose of reading, the ability to retain or recall information, select important points, interpret information, make general conclusions and judgments and relate knowledge to experience. Accurately group together and memorize your ideas. Determine your reading rate to comprehend by the difficulty level of the material, vocabulary, general background of knowledge, experience and importance of the reading material. Comprehending articles in a magazine in a doctor's office will probably differ from reading a textbook for a test you have in two days. Test your comprehension by creating an intelligence diagram from each chapter. Reflect on what you just read and write down the key points. Review the active reading section to improve comprehension.

Poets use language to create a powerful image or emotion. How does the poet use words to convey an emotion or a picture? Poets use metaphors and similes to convey the meaning, message or lesson of a poem. Poets use repetition of sounds, known as alliteration, to add color to the poem. Poets also personify animals with human characteristics in poems. Use the visual and emotional clues created through the poet's words to help you understand the poem's theme.

READING AND YOUR CHILD

Teach your child to enjoy reading by sharing books and stories with them. Read aloud with them. Listen to your child read every single day. Your child needs an audience. Set aside time for children to read by themselves. Work on phonics at home. Supply good books outside of school. Monitor and supplement the school's reading lists. Choose books that complement schoolwork. Expose your child to some classics. Read books and stories about your family's own heritage. Find books that relate to your child's interests. Talk to your child about what they have read. This helps build vocabulary, reviews the story and relates words to other experiences. Ask a few thought-provoking questions about the plot, characters or theme. This will sharpen comprehension and build appreciation for elements of literature such as theme and style. What did the author say to you? Read what your child reads to improve your conversations about literature and to be more helpful. Interacting with your children about what they read shows your interest in them. Keep your children reading during the summer. Visit the library. Try book clubs or magazine subscriptions. Start your own book club. Use reference works. Play word and letter games. Learn the origins of words. Read books from outstanding authors such as Anton Chekhov, Oscar Wilde, Robert Louis Stevenson, Washington Irving, Dorothy Sayers, Ernest Hemingway, James Cain, Charles Dickens, Aristotle, Agatha Christie, Jane Austen, Nathaniel Hawthorne, Jack London, Mark Twain, Jonathan Swift, Plato, Voltaire, William Shakespeare, William Faulkner, Leo Tolstoy, Daniel Defoe, James F. Cooper, Louisa Alcott, Edgar Allen Poe, Herman Melville, Walt Whitman, Dashiell Hammett, Ralph W. Emerson, T. S. Elliot, F. Scott Fitzgerald and Thomas Wolfe.

Writing Skills

Abbreviation

An abbreviation shortens the word or phrase by omitting letters.

An abbreviation generally ends with a period.

To prevent confusion, spell out the original word followed by the abbreviated word in parentheses.

Abbreviate:

- ➢ Social titles: Mister (Mr.), unmarried woman (Miss), unknown marital status (Ms.), married woman (Mrs.), Junior (Jr.), Senior (Sr.)

- ➢ Titles of rank: Lieutenant Smith to Lt. Smith, Sergeant to Sgt., Captain to Capt., General to Gen.

- ➢ Titles: Honorable (Hon.), Reverend (Rev.); abbreviate the title if first and last name occurs in the title (Hon. Mary Smith, Rev. Jerry Johnson)

- ➢ Business: Ampersand (&), Brothers (Bros.), Incorporated (Inc.), Corporation (Corp.), Company (Co.); use abbreviation if in official name; otherwise, spell out business name

- ➢ Academic degrees: Bachelor of Arts (B.A.), Bachelor of Science (B.S.), Bachelor of Science in Electrical Engineering (B.S.E.E.), Bachelor of Law (LL.B.), Master of Arts (M.A.), Master of Business Administration (MBA), Master of Science (M.S.)

- ➢ Spell out academic, civil, military or religious titles if they use only a last name (Reverend Johnson, Lieutenant Smith).

- ➢ Professional titles: Attorney (Atty.), Doctor (Dr.), Doctor of Divinity (D.D.), Doctor of Dental Science (D.D.S.), Doctor of Education (Ed. D.), Doctor of Philosophy (Ph.D.), Doctor of Law (LL.D.)

- Time: ante meridiam or before noon (A.M. or a.m.), post meridiam or after noon (P.M. or p.m.). Periods are optional if using small caps (7 AM).

- Historical periods: Before Christ (B.C.), Before the Common Era (B.C.E.), Common Era (C.E.) or anno Domini (A.D., beginning of calendar time)

- Addresses or location: Avenue (Ave.), Boulevard (Blvd.), Canyon (Cyn.), Circle (Cir.), Court (Ct.), Drive (Dr.), Lane (Ln.), Point (Pt.), Road (Rd.), Route (Rte.), Square (Sq.) and Street (St.)

- States (capital letters, no period): Alabama (AL), Alaska (AK), Arizona (AZ), Arkansas (AR), California (CA), Colorado (CO), Connecticut (CT), Delaware (DE), District of Columbia (DC), Florida (FL), Georgia (GA), Hawaii (HI), Idaho (ID), Illinois (IL), Indiana (IN), Iowa (IA), Kansas (KS), Kentucky (KY), Louisiana (LA), Maine (ME), Maryland (MD), Massachusetts (MA), Michigan (MI), Minnesota (MN), Mississippi (MS), Missouri (MO), Montana (MT), Nebraska (NB), Nevada (NV), New Hampshire (NH), New Jersey (NJ), New Mexico (NM), New York (NY), North Carolina (NC), North Dakota (ND), Ohio (OH), Oklahoma (OK), Oregon (OR), Pennsylvania (PA), Rhode Island (RI), South Carolina (SC), South Dakota (SD), Tennessee (TN), Texas (TX), Utah (UT), Vermont (VT), Virginia (VA), Washington (WA), West Virginia (WV), Wisconsin (WI) and Wyoming (WY)

- Latin expressions: *exempli gratia*, for example (e.g.), et cetera (etc.), and others (et al.) *id est*, that is (i.e.)

- Do not use **et cetera** with **and**

- Do not use **etc.** at the end of a list or series introduced by the phrases **such as** or **for example** because these phrases already indicate other things of the same category not named.

- Use **for example** or **such as** instead of **e.g.**

- Measurements: ampere (amp.), atmosphere (atm.), barrel (bbl), British thermal unit (Btu), calorie (cal), dozen (dz.), feet (ft.), gallon (gal.), gram (g), horsepower (hp), inch (in.), mile (mi.), ounce (oz.), pint (pt.), pound (lb.), quart (qt.), tablespoon (tbs.), teaspoon (tsp.), yard (yd.). For the singular and plural measurement, use the same abbreviated form.

➤ Do not follow metric abbreviations with a period such as kilogram (kg), kilometer (km) meter (m) and other metric quantities such as millimeter (mm) and centimeter (cm).

➤ Months of the year: January (Jan.), February (Feb.), March (Mar.), April (Apr.), May, June, July, August (Aug.), September (Sept.), October (Oct.), November (Nov.) and December (Dec.)

➤ An acronym using a capitalized first letter for each word of an organization, term or thing without periods: Self-Contained Underwater Breathing Apparatus (SCUBA), North American Treaty Organization (NATO), Federal Bureau of Investigation (FBI), United Nations (UN), collect on delivery (COD), As Soon As Possible (ASAP), United and Strengthening America by Providing Appropriate Tools Required to Intercept and Obstruct Terrorism (USA PATRIOT). Use an acronym as a study aid.

➤ Time: hour (hr.), second (sec.), year (yr.)

Write out numbers if they are fewer than three words; otherwise, use figures.

Write out round millions (one million) and billions; this avoids a string of zeroes.

Use figures in dates, addresses, decimals, percentages, page numbers and hours followed by **a.m.** or **p.m.**

Write out hours when not including minutes, followed by o'clock (seven o'clock).

Make the plural of figures by adding apostrophe **s** (three 7's).

Write the year as a figure and before the following date with an en dash to show range (1997–99).

Abbreviate pages with pp. and use en dash to show range (pp. 100–05).

ADJECTIVES

Adjectives describe nouns or pronouns (subject).

Descriptive adjectives answer what kind (red apple).

Qualitative adjectives answer how much (sweetest apple).

Demonstrative adjectives answer which one (that/this apple or these/those apples).

Use **this** and **that** with singular nouns. Use **these** and **those** with plural nouns.

A demonstrative adjective, the noun and the object of the preposition should agree in number.

Quantitative adjectives answer how many (one or first apple).

Relative adjectives answer possession (whose apple). Relative adjectives help link dependent clauses to main clauses. Interrogative adjectives answer which or what (which apple). Possessive adjectives, **her, his, its, my, our, their** and **your,** modify nouns.

Put adjectives before the noun, attribution position (the green apple).

Put adjectives after the noun, predicate position (the apple looks green).

Put the quantifying adjective before the descriptive adjective when they appear together to describe the noun (two red apples).

Form proper adjectives from proper nouns (American music, Chinese tea).

Two or more adjectives describing a noun form a compound adjective (well-designed car).

Indefinite adjectives describe general quantities of nouns (**all, any, some, many** apples).

Use a plural verb when indefinite adjectives modify plural count nouns (some apples are on the floor). Use a singular verb when an indefinite adjective modifies an uncountable mass noun (some oil is on the floor). Since *some* represents a mass noun, use singular verb, **is.** Use **any** with negative sentences or questions. (She does not have any money. Do you have any money?)

Use an adjective after a linking verb, known as a predicate adjective or adjective complement, which completes the meaning of the linking verb by describing the subject.

(They were healthy. **Healthy**, adjective complement, describes **they**. Bob is a teacher. **A teacher** represents a predicate nominative, a noun or pronoun that renames or identifies the subject (Bob) following a linking verb.)

Action verbs require adverbs, not adjectives (Bob drives cautiously).

Prepositional phrases, verbal phrases and adjective dependent clauses also describe a noun.

To modify a direct object after a transitive verb, use an adjective, an objective complement (Bob opened the heavy door. **Heavy** modifies the direct object **door**).

Use articles, **a, an** or **the,** as adjectives (an apple, a bird, the apple).

COMPARATIVE ADJECTIVES:

The base form, or positive form, of an adjective does not show comparison or differences in degree (cold weather). The comparative degree of an adjective or adverb compares two things and adds **er** to the base form of an adjective (colder weather). To compare three or more items, add the suffix **est** to the base form of an adjective (coldest weather). Use **er** or **est** with one and two syllable adjectives. Use **more** to form the comparative with two or more syllable adjectives and **most** to form the superlative. Do not use **er** and **more** or **est** and **most** together. Add **more** to **ly** words that answer **how**. Add **er** or **more** to **ly** words that answer **what kind**. When comparing three or more items, add **est** or **most** to the detailed words (more entertaining movie, most entertaining movie).

Adjectives with irregular forms of comparison:

Positive (Base)	Comparative	Superlative
good	better	best
well	better	best
bad	worse	worst
badly	worse	worst
far	farther	farthest
far	further	furthest
late	later	later or latest
little (amount)	less, lesser	least
many	more	most
much	more	most
some	more	most

For the comparative and superlative degree for the antonyms of **more** and **most**, use **less** and **least**. **Less** refers to a quantity that forms a whole, which cannot be counted or interchanged. **Fewer** represents items counted or interchanged. When you compare one item in a group with the rest of the group, use **other** or **else** to differentiate the item from the group. When comparing similar items, finish the comparison by naming the noun for each comparison in the sentence. (This apple tastes better than the other apples.)

Use **bad** as an adjective. Use **badly** as an adverb. Use **good** as an adjective. Use **well** as an adjective to describe good health and use well as an adverb to describe anything else.

The company makes a good car; it runs well. He has a good voice; he speaks well. **Good** modifies **car**, so it is an adjective. **Well** modifies the verb **runs**, so it is an adverb. In the second sentence, **good** modifies the noun **voice**, so it is an adjective. **Well** modifies the verb **speaks**, so it is an adverb.

Use superlatives without comparing items (best wishes or deepest regrets).

Use only one negative word to express a negative idea. Examples of negative words are **no, never, not, none, nothing, hardly, scarcely** and **barely**.

Present and past participles may represent adjectives (rising sun, completed project, sunken submarine).

Examples of Adjectives:

Abhorrent, acceptable, adept, aerial, affirmative, aggressive, airtight, alert, ambiguous, analytic, apparent, aquatic, arable, assertive, atrocious, austere, averse, awkward, axial, azure, bad, beautiful, big, black, bold, brash, budgetary, cagey, celestial, characteristic, circular, clamorous, coarse, crass, curious, cynical, daft, deaf, diagnostic, docile, dreary, dull, dwarf, dynamic, eager, eccentric, edible, efficient, egregious, either, elaborate, emphatic, engaged, equitable, erroneous, essential, ethical, euphoric, evil, exact, fabulous, feeble, fictitious, flaccid, foolish, fragile, fugitive, gallant, generous, ghastly, gigantic, glossy, gold, grandiose, gullible, gymnastic, habitable, healthy, hideous, homogenous, huge, hypnotic, identical, ignorant, illusory, imaginary, inappropriate, ironclad, jaunty, jealous, jittery, jocular, jubilant, kaput, keen, khaki, kind, knowledgeable, lackluster, lemon, liable, loathsome, lucrative, lymphatic, magical, mediocre, mild, modern, multiple, mythical, naïve, necessary, nice, noble, nutrient, obedient, odious, offensive, oily, old, ominous, onerous, opaque, orange, ostensible, other, outrageous, overpowering, pale, pectoral, phobic, picturesque, pleasant, poignant, pragmatic, pristine, prolific, pseudo, pubescent, quaint, quasi, quick, quirky, quixotic, radiant, ready, righteous, rocky, rugged, sad, silent, sour, sparse, stark, suave, sweet, sympathetic, tan, teak, tight, toned, treacherous, turbid, twelve, ugly, under, uphill, vague, vehement, visible, volatile, vulnerable, warm, west, wheezy, wild, wonderful, wretched, yellow, zealous, zonal

Adverbs

Adverbs modify or describe verbs (action), adjectives, other adverbs or clauses.

Adverbs answer when, at what time; where, at what location (down, up, here, there); how, by what manner (quickly, slowly, fast); how much or to what extent.

Add **ly** to an adjective to form an adverb.

Position the adverb before or after the intended verb in a sentence.

You may place an adverb between a helping verb and main verb. If the adverb modifies only the main verb, then place the adverb immediately before the main verb. (The book has been incorrectly written.)

Do not place an adverb phrase between compound verbs.

To emphasize the adverb, place it before the subject (**Clearly**, he felt sad).

Examples of Adverbs:

above, about, absolutely, actually, accurately, adversely, after, afterward, already, almost, around, as, aside, audibly, aversely, away, awhile, awkwardly, back, backward, badly, before, behind, beneath, besides, best, between, beyond, blindly, boldly, briefly, briskly, by, certainly, cheaply, clearly, close, cyclically, dangerously, dearly, densely, diagonally, differently, down, downward, duly, each, early, either, elsewhere, especially, eternally, even, ever, exceedingly, fairly, faithfully, far, fast, fiercely, foremost, gently, gingerly, gladly, gradually, habitually, hard, hardly, heavily, hence, here, historically, honorably, horribly, how, however, humbly, illegibly, incidentally, indefinitely, inside, inward, jointly, just, keenly, kindly, last, late, lately, legally, less, likely, long, low, mainly, maybe, mildly, moderately, more, moreover, most, much, namely, naturally, near, neatly, never, nevertheless, next, no, normally, nothing, nowhere, oddly, officially, often, once, only, openly, orderly, originally, outside, partially, particularly, past, patiently, perhaps, personally, politely, practically, quick, quite, rarely, rather, sideward, simply, since, some, somehow, sometime, soon, soundly, specially, spiritually, still, slow, so tomorrow, still, sternly, such, suddenly, then, today, too, true, twice, unduly, unjustly, very, vernally, vicariously, warily, well, what, when, where, wherever, why, within, without, yearly, yesterday, yet

Use the **ly** adverb form when someone feels, tastes, hears or smells something (hands, tongue, ears, nose). The cat sniffed (smell) the food cautiously (how). She tasted (taste) the juice enthusiastically (how). They heard the dogs bark loudly (how much).

Conjunctive adverbs, which act like conjunctions, link two independent clauses with a semicolon followed by a conjunctive adverb, followed by a comma and then the second clause. Conjunctive adverbs show relationships such as examples, continuation, contrast and comparison. (Karen wrote a book about animals; consequently, her income increased.) Examples of conjunctive adverbs are: **accordingly, also, again, besides, consequently, finally, for example, furthermore, however, indeed, moreover, nevertheless, nonetheless, on the other hand, otherwise, therefore, then** and **thus.**

Interrogative adverbs ask questions: **where, when, why, how.**

Examples of numeric adverbs are **once** or **twice.**

Prepositional phrases, verbal phrases and adverbial dependent clauses modify verbs too.

For comparative degree adverbs with one syllable, add **more** to the **ly** word (more friendly). For superlative degree adverbs with two or more syllables, add **most** to the **ly** word (most cautiously). Use **less** and **least** as antonyms of **more** and **most.**

Agreement

A subject must agree with its verb in number and person.

A singular subject requires a singular verb.

Plural subjects require a plural verb.

Abstract nouns such as **news, economics, social studies, ham and eggs** require a singular verb.

A prepositional phrase or clause between a subject and its verb does not affect subject verb agreement.

Titles require a singular verb.

Singular subjects connected by **either ... or**, **neither ... nor** and **not only ... but also**, require a singular verb because these connecting words choose only one item.

Most measurements require a singular verb.

Collective nouns (indefinite pronouns) such as **anyone, someone, everyone** that function as a single subject require a singular verb. Other collective nouns such as **committee, flock, herd, team, audience, assembly, team** or **club** may represent a plural or singular subject depending on the meaning. If the subject (antecedent) consists of two or more pronouns connected by **or, nor, not only, but, also** or correlative conjunctions such as **either ... or, neither ... nor,** the verb agrees with the noun closer to the pronoun (antecedent). **Many a, part, series** and **portion** require a singular verb. **There, here** or **where** at the beginning of a sentence usually requires you to invert the word order to find the subject, verb and verb agreement. Add an **s** or **es** to the third-person singular form of most verbs to form the singular. (He increases the cost.) Do not add an **s** to the third-person singular verb form to form the plural. (They increase the cost.)

A pronoun agrees with its antecedent in number, person and gender.

Use the noun before using the pronoun to prevent confusion.

Use a plural pronoun when the antecedents are joined by **and**.

Use a singular pronoun if the nouns are preceded by **each** or **every**.

Inverted sentences may result in the subject following the verb.

Do not let clauses and phrases cloud the subject and verb agreement of a sentence.

A compound antecedent joined by **or** or **nor** is singular if both subjects are singular and is plural if both subjects are plural. If one of the antecedents is plural and one singular, the pronoun agrees with the nearer antecedent. If two antecedents refer to the same person, use a singular pronoun. Use the pronoun **his** for the masculine person. Use the pronoun **her** for the female person.

Indefinite pronouns can be singular or plural. Indefinite pronouns ending in **body** such as **anybody, somebody** or **nobody** require a singular verb or singular pronoun if the above nouns represent antecedents. **All, any, more, most, none** or **some** represent a singular or plural subject depending on whether they are used with a mass noun or a count noun.

For indefinite antecedents such as **anyone,** try to use a plural pronoun or both feminine and masculine pronouns.

Do not use a plural pronoun with a singular antecedent.

When the word **number** represents a specific number, use a singular verb. (The number of the team is five.)

When the word **number** represents an approximate number, use a plural verb. (A number of team members were waiting for the bus.)

The antecedents of the relative pronouns **that, which** and **who** will determine a singular or plural verb.

Trousers, pants and scissors require a plural verb.

A singular subject followed by a clause or phrase containing a plural noun requires a singular verb. (**One** of the birds we tested **is** diagnosed with a virus.) Do not use the subject complement as the subject.

Apostrophes (')

An apostrophe and an **s** ('s) at the end of word shows possession (car's).

To decide whether an apostrophe goes before or after the **s**, substitute and test it (woman's dresses, dresses belong to a woman).

Let the sound of the construction determine whether you use the apostrophe or **of the** for inanimate objects or when you concentrate on an activity rather than on a person.

To show individual possession with connecting nouns, provide possession form for each noun (Bob's and Amy's cats).

To form possession of compound nouns or hyphenated words put the apostrophe **s** on the last word (father-in-law's or Bob and Amy's cat).

With singular nouns ending in **s**, add an apostrophe and an **s** (hostess's).

With plural nouns ending in **s**, add an apostrophe after the **s** (girls').

Indefinite pronouns that do not end in **s** or with an **s** or a **z** sound, add apostrophe and **s** (anyone's).

With plural nouns not ending in **s**, add an apostrophe and an **s** (women's).

Use an apostrophe and **s** to show the plural of a letter such as **p's** and **q's**.

Do not use an apostrophe with possessive pronouns (my, mine, our, ours, your, yours, theirs, his, her, hers, its their, theirs, and whose).

When you contract words, add an apostrophe in the space of the omitted letters (**they are** to **they're**, **will not** to **won't**, **cannot** to **can't** and **it is** to **it's**).

Add an apostrophe to show that numbers have been left out of a date such as '80s and '90s.

Don't confuse contractions with possessive pronouns such as **it's** and **its**, **you're** and **your**, **they're** and **their**, **who's** and **whose**.

Use apostrophe and **s** to show the plural of a number (**three's**).

Use an apostrophe and **s** to show the plural of a word referred to as a word. (The sentence had six **the's.**)

Don't try to form the possessive of the title of a play, a book or a film. Reword the sentence instead.

Use an apostrophe to make plurals of words that do not usually have a plural.

Add apostrophe and **s** to possessive adjectives for periods of time or amounts of money (month's vacation, dollar's value).

Make the plurals of digits and letters by adding an apostrophe and **s** (**10's**, **if's**, **and's** or **but's**).

Do not use an apostrophe to form the plural if an abbreviation is in all capital letters or ends with a capital letter (IOUs).

Use an apostrophe to form the plural if an abbreviation contains more than one period (M.D.'s or Ph.D.'s).

Written out numbers do not require an apostrophe.

ARTICLES

Definite and indefinite articles, considered adjectives, limit or make the word they modify more exact.

The indefinite article does not represent a specific person, place or thing.

Use the indefinite article **a** when the next word or abbreviation begins with a consonant or consonant sound (a bird, a union).

Use indefinite article **an** when the next word or abbreviation begins with a vowel or vowel sound (an apple, an MBA).

The definite article **the** refers to a specific thing (the cat, the table). Use **the** with an adjective without a noun (the sick, the poor, the rich). Do not use **the** with names of people or places unless States, Kingdom or Republic represents part of the place (the United States, the United Kingdom, the Dominican Republic). Use **the** with plural places, with plural names, canals, oceans, seas and rivers (the Pacific Ocean, the Smiths, the Joneses). Use **the** with an adjective and noun combination (the Palace of Fine Arts).

Do not use **the** with names ending in **'s, s** or names of companies (Lloyds Bank, McDonalds). An article that applies to all the members of a series must either be used before the first item or else repeated before each item (the **a, b,** and **c**; otherwise, use the **a**, the **b** and the **c**). This same rule applies for prepositions.

BRACKETS [ ]

Use brackets to enclose editorial comments, clarify information, insert a remark into a direct quotation from another source or set off a parenthetical item within parentheses (and Bob **[1920–1995]** started the solar project).

Use brackets around the word **sic** to show the original writer or speaker made an error in the quotation but that you are quoting verbatim.

CAPITALIZATION

Capitalize:

➢ The first word of a sentence. Spell out a number that starts a sentence (One).

➢ The first word of a complete sentence or question after a colon. Do not capitalize first word of a subordinate clause after a colon.

➢ The first word of a direct quoted sentence, but not a quoted phrase, fragment of a quote or indirect quote (discourse).

- He said, "Let's go to the theater."

- She said, "Help me find my car keys."

- "Blood clots," the nurse explained, "can cause death."

➢ The first word of a formal introduction.

➢ The first word on a line of poetry.

- ➢ First word in the greeting of a letter (Dear John:).

- ➢ First word in a complimentary close of a letter (Sincerely yours, Best regards).

- ➢ First word of each item in an outline.

- ➢ First word of a completed sentence contained as a numbered item.

- ➢ The first letter of the first word in titles of books, films, plays, paintings, newspapers and magazines; the first letter of all other words in the title except articles (a, an, the), conjunctions (and, but, if) or prepositions with fewer than four letters (at, in, on, of). Example: Learning, Reading and Writing Strategies for the Motivated Student.

- ➢ Titles before a person's name such as Dr., Mr., Vice President or Professor.

- ➢ Do not capitalize appositives following proper nouns, except for epithets.

- ➢ Military officers, religious titles, officials, politicians or professions (Father, Sister and Captain, President Abraham Lincoln).

- ➢ Abbreviations that appear after a person's name such as Jr., Ph.D., M.D., if the same unabbreviated words are capitalized (Jack Jones, Junior).

- ➢ Names of books and plays and underline or italicize magazine titles.

- ➢ Geographical places and geographic divisions or sections of the country (Europe, Asia, North America, Middle East, Orient, the South).

- ➢ Geographic features when part of a proper name (Rocky Mountains, not mountains).

- ➢ Titles used in direct address. ("Doctor, I have a pain in my side.")

- Names of specific historical events, eras, specific periods of time and documents (Renaissance, Great Depression, Revolutionary War, Declaration of Independence).

- Names of languages, nationalities, countries, ethnic groups and races (Dutch, England, American Indian, Chinese).

- Religions and references to the Supreme Being (Allah, God) including the pronouns referring to the Supreme Being. (It is He who hath created us all.)

- Bible, if it refers to the Christian Scriptures.

- The first letter of each word of a person's name. (Some foreign language names have exceptions, such as Van de Camp.)

- Proper nouns and proper adjectives in a hyphenated proper adjective.

- Brand names and trademarks.

- Names of specific organizations, institutions, associations and famous buildings.

- Internal divisions and departments (Faculty, Accounting Department, Board of Directors).

- Days, months and holidays.

- Abbreviations for time.

- Words **I** and **O**!

- Letters that represent names or indicate shapes (U-turn, vitamin A, X-ray).

- Names of specific animal classes, families and orders, but not species (Enhydra lutris).

- Planets, constellations, stars; capitalize earth, sun and moon only when used with planet names.

- Titles of parents and relatives not preceded by a possessive word and when you don't use their personal names. (We saw Father, Mother, Uncle Sam and Aunt Jane.)

- ➢ A compass point that identifies a specific area of the country (Southwest, South, Northeast); do not capitalize direction (north, south, east or west).

- ➢ The next letter if the name begins with Mc, O or St. (McDonald, O'Reily, St. Joseph).

- ➢ If a name begins with la, le, Mac, van, von, de or D, clarify for specific spelling.

- ➢ Chapters of books, rooms in a building (Chapter 6, Room 3).

- ➢ Abbreviations B.C. and A.D.

- ➢ Names of transportation (United Airlines, *Titanic*, Amtrak).

Don't capitalize the prefix attached to a proper adjective unless the prefix refers to a nationality (All-American, pre–World War II).

Don't combine the abbreviations Mr., Mrs. or Ms. with an abbreviation for a professional or academic title.

Don't capitalize seasons (fall, winter, spring or summer).

Don't capitalize minor divisions within large units (page 5, verse 7 or seat 22).

CLAUSE

A clause, a group of words, adds logic, unity and cohesion to a sentence by sharpening meaning, linking or combining related ideas or adding detail to the subject, object or verb.

Clauses avoid monotony, create brevity and provide appropriate emphasis.

A clause functions as an adjective, adverb, adverb clause, subject, direct object, indirect object, object of a preposition, noun, predicate nominative, complement or appositive to create more effective sentences.

An independent clause (main clause) contains a subject and a predicate and forms a complete thought; therefore, it is a sentence. The independent clause should contain the more important idea or emphasis in the sentence.

A dependent clause (subordinate clause) helps develop, enhance, and adds variety, conciseness and emphasis to the main or independent clause. A dependent clause does not represent a complete thought; therefore, it is not a sentence. A dependent clause defines the relationship between the main idea and secondary idea (logic, time, place) of a sentence. Use a dependent clause to describe, explain, amplify, illustrate, or represent a condition or consequence in relation to the main clause. Substitute a series of simple or compound sentences with a dependent clause. The dependent clause answers where, why, when, to what extent, under what conditions or in what manner.

Introduce clauses with coordinating conjunctions, subordinating conjunctions, conjunctive adverbs, relative pronouns, conjunctions or relative pronouns.

Subordinating conjunctions (although, as, because, even though, if, include, since, so, though, when, where, while, unless, until) link a dependent clause with the main independent clause by expressing the relationship between the two clauses forming a complex sentence. When you start the subordinate clause with a subordinating conjunction, the main clause will follow to complete the idea. When a subordinating conjunction introduces the dependent clause before the independent clause, separate the clauses by a comma. You may not need a comma if the subordinating conjunction does not start the sentence.

Do not use prepositions to introduce a clause such as **like**; use **as** or **as if**.

Some conjunctions express a condition (**even if, if, provided that** or **unless**).

Some conjunctions express reason (**as, as if**, or **because**).

Some conjunctions express choice (**rather than, than** or **whether**).

Some conjunctions express contrast (**although, but, even though** or **though**).

Some conjunctions express location (**where** or **wherever**).

Some conjunctions express time (**after, as soon as, before, once, when, whenever** or **while**).

An **adjective clause**, a subordinate clause, describes nouns or pronouns in the sentence.

An adjective clause that begins with a relative pronoun, which functions as an adjective, direct object, object of the preposition or subject (**who, whom, whose, which**, or **that**) creates a **relative clause.** Carefully place the adjective clause close to the noun or pronoun to reduce any confusion. Use **who, whom, whoever,** or **whomever** when you refer to people.

Use **which** or **that** when you refer to a thing or an animal.

A **noun clause** functions as a noun. A noun clause may omit the words **which** or **whom**, the subject or the verb. Interrogative and relative pronouns frequently introduce noun clauses.

A **restrictive clause** limits the meaning of what it modifies (subject, noun), and if removed, would change the meaning of the sentence and does not require commas. A nonrestrictive clause does not limit the meaning of what it modifies, and if removed, would not change the meaning of the sentence but provides additional information and is set off by commas. Use a comma to separate a restrictive clause from a nonrestrictive clause. Use **that** for restrictive relative clauses and **which** for nonrestrictive clauses.

An **elliptical clause,** an adverb, adjective or noun clause, clearly implies some words (subject or verb) rather than states them. The omitted words should represent the same words of the main clause; otherwise, there could be a possibility of confusion between clauses.

An **adverb clause** may omit the subject or verb. Introduce an adverb clause with subordinating conjunctions. Do not use an adverb clause as the subject in a sentence. If the adverb clause follows the main clause, do not separate clauses with a comma. If

44

the adverb clause precedes the main clause, then use a comma between the clauses.

Add **ing** to a word to form an **ing** clause. (Bob injured his foot **playing** basketball.) If the sentence starts with an **ing clause,** add a comma followed by the main clause. (**Playing** basketball, Bob injured his foot.)

CLICHÉS

A cliché, a trite expression, lacks uniqueness and potentially blocks specific details of your intended thought.

CLIPPED WORD

Cut off the beginning or ending of a word to shorten the word; usually no period because it's not an abbreviation.

COLON (:)

A colon represents a stop or points toward something that follows which finishes the idea.

Use a colon when you list items in a complete sentence. (I like to eat these vegetables: carrots, lettuce and cucumbers.) Do not use a colon if the list completes the meaning of the sentence. (The vegetables I like to eat are carrots, lettuce and cucumbers.)

Use a colon:

- ➢ To link independent clauses when the second clause modifies the first clause

- ➢ To end the main clause and introduce additional information, changes or explain further the main clause

- ➢ Between a title and subtitle (*The Exciting Adventures of Hydra and Muste Otter: Life in the Big Sea*)

- ➤ To separate hours from minutes (11:30)

- ➤ To distinguish a chapter from a verse in a Biblical citation such as Psalm 23:1

- ➤ Between volume and page number (*Encyclopedia Britannica* V: One)

- ➤ To separate bibliographic entries (New York: Parker Publishing)

- ➤ After the salutation of a business letter (Dear Mr. Kingston:)

- ➤ Before a long quotation; place the colon outside the quotation

- ➤ To introduce a direct quotation; put the colon outside the quotation

When quoting material that ends in a colon, drop the colon and replace it with ellipses (*not* answers:", *use* answers …").

The colon substitutes for the words **namely** or **that is** in a sentence.

Capitalize the first letter after a colon if the quoted material originally began with a capital letter.

If subordinate information follows a colon, use a lowercase letter following the colon.

Use a colon after a completed sentence to introduce a formal resolution or question.

Use a colon to indicate mathematical ratios or substances (water-to-sand ratio 7:5).

Comma

A comma denotes a pause in the sentence, especially with long phrases.

A comma separates and encloses phrases (introductory prepositional phrase, phrases in apposition) or clauses (introductory subordinated clause, separate main and subordinate clauses, nonrestrictive clause or phrase).

Use two commas to enclose nonrestrictive clauses. For example, enclose a nonrestrictive participating phrase: The electrician, working quickly and efficiently, finished early.

Do not use commas for restrictive clauses.

You may omit a comma for short introductory clauses or phrases related to the main clause.

Do not use two commas to enclose parentheses in the middle of a sentence. A parenthetical phrase can be eliminated without changing the meaning of a sentence and if removed, should not result in two commas being together.

A comma clarifies sentence meaning to prevent misreading, eliminate ambiguity or potential confusion.

Use a comma:

  ➢ To separate the main clause from a sentence fragment

  ➢ After the greeting of an informal letter (Dear George,) or at the close of any letter (Sincerely yours,)

  ➢ To separate a name from a degree or title (John Doe, Ph.D.)

  ➢ To set off interrupting transitional words, phrases and expressions

  ➢ To set off words of a direct address or quotation such as a dialogue from its source unless parentheses follow the quotation (The teacher said, "Do your homework.")

> To set off words that give additional information about the preceding or following word or expression such as adjectives that modify a noun separately such as salty, humid air or an appositive, a word or group of words immediately following a noun or pronoun providing more information about the noun or pronoun

You can eliminate a comma after a nonrestrictive modifier that will not create confusion.

Do not use a comma or commas if the items in a series are connected by conjunctions.

Do not use a comma for an indirect quote or address (discourse).

You may put a comma before **and** in a series of items.

A comma follows a parenthetical expression unless parentheses surrounds a digit or letter to enumerate a series (George's new house, in my opinion, reminds me of a medieval castle).

Use a comma before adverb conjunctions (**however**).

Use a comma to separate parts of a compound sentence.

Do not use a comma between a compound subject or predicate consisting of only two elements.

Use a comma before the coordinating conjunction (and, but, for, or, nor, so, yet) located between independent clauses of a sentence. Do not put a comma after a coordinating conjunction. Do not put a comma before a coordinating conjunction that links only a phrase. Do not put a comma between independent clauses without a coordinating conjunction. Substitute a semicolon for a comma and coordinating conjunction.

When a conjunctive adverb connects two independent clauses, a semicolon precedes the conjunctive adverb followed by a comma (**however, nevertheless, therefore, consequently, moreover, certainly, indeed, and the like**). For example, I like your idea; however, look at this new information. As an alternative, you could create two sentences or subordinate one clause to the main clause with a comma.

Do not use a comma if a word or phrase does not interrupt the continuity of thought.

Put a comma between city and state of an address (Los Gatos, CA).

Put a comma between the day of the month and the year (September 11, 2001).

Do not use a comma in the day-month-year format (4 July 2004).

Use a comma to separate a geographical location within another geographical location (San Francisco, California, United States).

Use a comma to separate thousands, millions, etc. (1,000, 1,000,000).

Cumulative adjectives do not require a comma (two small apples). Adjectives of equal importance require a comma (red, large apples). Can each adjective stand alone with the noun or pronoun? If so, then add a comma between each word. Reversing the adjectives will help determine equal importance—does it still make sense?

Multiple sets of cumulative adjectives do require a comma.

Do not use a comma for identifying words that interrupt a main clause in a question.

Use a comma when the title comes directly after an introductory expression that gives additional information or acts as a bridge.

Use a semicolon to separate phrases or clauses in a series when one or more of the phrases or clauses contain commas (George Washington, President; John Adams, Vice President; and Benjamin Franklin, Ambassador).

Reversed name order requires a comma (Jefferson, Thomas).

Use commas to separate items in a series (The company produces oil, gas, coal and chemicals). Do not put a comma before the first or after the last item of a series.

Separate certain elements of a footnote and bibliography (Sunshine Press, 1999, p. 20).

Use a comma for introductory interjection (**oh, well, why, indeed, yes** or **no**). For example, Yes, I agree. No, I do not agree.

Do not use a comma with a period, question mark, exclamation mark or dash, except with abbreviations.

Do not use a comma between a subject and verb or between a verb and its object.

A comma sometimes replaces a verb in certain elliptical constructions (some were punctual; others, late). A comma replaces **were**.

Use commas to separate contrasting ideas in a sentence.

Use commas to separate words or phrases that interrupt the flow of the sentence.

Use commas to separate a person addressed in the sentence.

COMPLEMENT

A word, phrase or clause used in a predicate of a sentence to complete the meaning of the sentence is called a complement.

A noun or noun equivalent that receives the action of a transitive verb answers the question **what** or **whom** after the verb.

> John built a business (noun).
> I like to work (verbal).
> I like it (pronoun).
> I like what I saw (noun clause).

A direct object completes the sense of a transitive verb.

An indirect object (reveals something about the object of its transitive verb, and is either a noun or an adjective) completes the meaning of a transitive verb and the verb's direct object.

A noun or noun equivalent occurs with a direct object after certain kinds of transitive verbs (**give, wish, cause** and **tell**). The noun equivalent answers the question **to whom** or **for whom** or **to what** or **for what**.

A **subjective complement** completes the meaning of the subject and follows a linking verb rather than a transitive verb describing the subject, and is either a noun or an adjective.

> He is a doctor (noun).
> She is sick (adjective).

An **objective complement** completes the meaning of a transitive verb's object by revealing something about the object, and is either a noun or an adjective. See Objects section for examples.

CONJUNCTIONS

Conjunctions connect words or groups of words (phrases or clauses) to show cause (results or possibilities), link ideas, reinforce the negative, contrast ideas or signal connections between parallel or closely related ideas.

Use coordinating conjunctions (**for, nor, but, or, yet, so**) to link independent clauses (identical function or equal importance).

Coordinating conjunction	Meaning	Function
for, because	because	to show cause, reason
and	also	to link or join ideas
nor	negative	to reinforce negative
but	however	to contrast ideas
or	choice, select	to show possibilities
yet	however	to contrast
so, accordingly, due to this	therefore	to show result

Two or more singular subjects joined by **or** or **nor** usually take a singular verb. When a sentence contains a singular and plural subject, the verb agrees with the nearest subject.

If commas occur within independent clauses, precede the coordinating conjunction with a semicolon.

Correlative conjunctions (coordinating conjunctions) used in pairs, link similar words or groups of words (both ... and, either ... or, neither ... nor, not only ... but also, whether ... or, not ... but).

Or follows **either**; **nor** always follows **neither**.

Paired words should follow logically by ideas of equal weight and similar construction.

Other correlative expressions link chronologically such as first, second, third, etc., which should follow the same grammatical construction (parallel sentence elements).

Use **subordinating conjunctions** to link adverbial or dependent clauses to the main or independent clause.

Do not use subordinating conjunctions to link independent clauses.

Subordinating Conjunction	Relationship
as, because	cause, reason
whether, rather than	choice
even if, if, unless, provided that, though, as soon as, as long as	condition
though, even though, although, nevertheless, nonetheless, yet, however, on the other hand, than, so, so what, in order that, that	contrast
wherever, where, nearly, in the distance, here, there, at the side, next to, adjacent, in the front, in the back, once, whenever, since, until	location
naturally, granted, certainly, sure	agreement
in addition to, and besides, further, furthermore, next, then, finally, moreover	addition
for example, for instance, namely, specifically	example
first, finally, second, secondly, third, fourth, next, then, subsequently, immediately, later, eventually, in the future, currently, now, during, meanwhile, before, soon, afterward, at length, since, until, when, while, after	time

Since emphasizes circumstances or conditions rather than cause and effect.

Join two independent clauses by putting a semicolon before a conjunctive adverb and then a comma (**however, moreover, therefore, further, then, consequently, besides, also, accordingly** or **thus**).

In as much as, implies concession or a true statement in view of the circumstances.

DASH (——)

Combine two hyphens without a space to form a dash (also known as an em dash because it is the width of a capital "M").

A dash creates a break or change from the flow of thought, emphatic pause or contrast in the sentence, which adds information but not necessarily to complete a grammatically correct sentence. A sentence should remain grammatically correct without the dash and the words contained within the dashes.

Use a dash to summarize the sentence.

A dash can serve like a period or comma, but do not use adjacent to either one. (A career as an archeologist—an ancient profession—lies in ruins.)

A dash can substitute for parentheses.

A quote with a dash or dashes remains inside the quotation marks. Added information that is not part of a quote remains outside the quotation marks.

Use a dash before a final summarizing statement or before repetition that represents an afterthought.

Use dashes for clarity when commas appear within parentheses; this avoids the confusion of too many commas.

Use dashes to set off an explanatory or appositive series. (Three of the workers—Carol, Mark and Ann—could work today.)

Do not capitalize the first word after the dash except for proper nouns.

Use a dash to indicate omitted letters.

Use a dash to connect an introductory phrase to the rest of the sentence. (The heart, kidneys, liver, lungs—these organs help save lives for transplant recipients.)

Use a short dash, an en dash (dash with the width of a capital "N"):

> ➢ To join compound modifiers (United States–Russian Treaty, Northern Mexico–California border)
> ➢ Whenever a compound modifier combines with a participle (U.S. Senate–backed proposal, San Francisco–based business)
> ➢ To show a span of page numbers (pp. 169–79, the en dash replaces the preposition **to** or **through** [169 to 179])
> ➢ To join already hyphenated compounds (pre-election polls–post-election polls)
> ➢ To mark the space between dates in a chronological range (Lincoln's presidency [1861–1865], 5:00–6:00 pm)
> ➢ Between indexed numbers and letters (chart 15–A)

Dialogue

Dialogue represents the conversation among characters in a story. Dialogue includes dialect, which helps reveal a character's education level, geographic background, ethnic background, emotional state, level of diction, connotation level or motives.

Dialogue includes patterns of speech (fast or slow pace), slang, accents, euphemisms, dysphemisms, jargon or punctuation. Dialogue may reveal setting, events or actions.

Dialogue usually occurs (written or spoken) in broken sentences, fragments (prepositional or infinitive phrases) or questions.

Start a new paragraph for each change of speaker in a dialogue.

The more conversational the dialogue, the greater the reader will feel as if part of the story.

DIRECT OBJECT

A **direct object** is a noun or equivalent (gerund, infinitive, pronoun, noun clause) that names a person or thing that receives the action of a transitive verb.

A direct object answers the question **what** or **whom**.

DOCUMENTATION

Formal credit given to sources used or quoted in a research project, report, bibliography or footnote (recorded information, flowchart, engineering drawing, research, expert testimony).

EDIT

Check for correct content information.

Check for grammar, usage and mechanics (spelling, punctuation and capitalization).

Check for sentence fragments and run-ons.

Check for spelling (missing letters, extra letters, transposed letters, incorrect plurals, and homonym errors).

Usage:

> ➢ Errors in pronouns, such as who/whom
> ➢ Problems with subject-verb agreement
> ➢ Lack of clarity
> ➢ Wrong verb tense
> ➢ Double negatives

- ➢ Dangling modifiers
- ➢ Unnecessary words
- ➢ Misused adjectives and adverbs
- ➢ Sexist language
- ➢ Incorrect voice, active vs. passive voice
- ➢ Lack of parallel structure

Punctuation:

- ➢ Missing commas, question marks or periods
- ➢ Misused semicolon and colons
- ➢ Missing or misused apostrophes

Capitalization:

- ➢ Proper nouns and adjectives not capitalized
- ➢ Errors in title

Ellipses (...)

Ellipses, three spaced periods (...), represent omitted words or sentences from a direct quote or passage.

Omission of words should not detract from or alter the meaning of the sentence.

Do not use ellipses to start a sentence; omit the words and continue the quote with a lowercase letter.

Use a full line of periods across the page to indicate the omission of one or more paragraphs.

Use a period and ellipses **(. ...)** to indicate an omission at the end of a complete sentence.

Use a period and ellipses **(... .)** to indicate an omission at the end of an incomplete sentence.

Ellipses also represent a pause or hesitation within a sentence. (The lottery winning number is ... 21578.)

End marks (. / ? / !)

End marks consist of a period (.), question mark (?) and exclamation mark (!).

End a sentence with one of the end marks to complete the thought.

Use a period:

> ➢ To complete a sentence
> ➢ After a command
> ➢ After most abbreviations
> ➢ After an initial in names
> ➢ After each Roman numeral, letter or number in an outline
> ➢ To separate chapter from verse in the Bible (Genesis iii.2 or Mark vi.10)
> ➢ In decimal points (5.5%, 10.4)
> ➢ To end imperative sentences that are not emphatic enough for an exclamation mark
> ➢ To end polite requests with an assumed positive response
> ➢ Between dollars and cents ($4.50)
> ➢ Called a "leader," a row of periods is used to connect one item to another in a table of contents (see the table of contents of this book for an example)

Do not use periods for acronyms (IRS or NATO).

Place a period inside a quotation mark that ends a sentence.

If a complete sentence is within parentheses, put the period inside the closing parenthesis.

If an incomplete sentence is within parentheses, put the period after the closing parenthesis.

Drop your voice and pause after a period.

Do not substitute a comma for a period.

Use a question mark after a question (complete sentence not required).

Use question marks to separate items within an interrogative sentence. (Did you remember to shut the windows? Lock the door? Feed the dog?)

End an interrogative exclamatory statement with a question mark. (The work is finished?)

Place a question mark not part of a quotation after the quotation mark.

Use an exclamation mark to show strong emotion, surprise or emphasis at the end of a sentence.

Use an exclamation mark or a comma after an interjection. (**oh! wow!** or **hey!**)

Do not combine an exclamation mark with a period, comma or question mark.

If a sentence begins with a question word but does not ask a question, use an exclamation point or period. (What an idiotic statement!)

Essay Writing

A standard essay consists of an introductory paragraph, the body discussing each major point with a paragraph and concluding paragraph. Each new paragraph allows the reader to rest between ideas and builds on what the reader learned in previous paragraphs. Each section of an essay can vary in length depending on complexity and importance. Summarize a highly detailed previous paragraph, group of paragraphs or transition between complicated paragraphs with additional short paragraphs.

The introductory paragraph states your topic, theme, goal, purpose, position (broad, narrow, concentrated) and main points you will discuss. Add any general or background information to clarify your purpose, tone and mood of the essay. Express any limitations or parameters of your subject. Define any key terms. Will your essay provide a new perspective or discuss additional information about an existing topic? Explain your strategy or approach to logically present your information used in the body of the essay. Choose an approach suited for your reader, subject and essay objective. For example, start with a generalized theme or point of view and provide examples, facts or statistics to justify your position. For an opposing strategy, start with a narrow theme or point of view and provide strong evidence to generalize your position. Ask a question important to the reader and then answer the question in the body of your essay. State incidents, personal experiences, quotations from experts, humor, anecdotes, short narratives or problems. State interesting, startling, striking or unexpected facts to generate interest. Summarize results or statistics to emphasize your point or position. Indirectly introduce your topic and develop your point of view or purpose in your essay. Explain how you will evaluate or recommend action in the concluding paragraph. Start with an opposing point of view, and then reverse to your point of view. Explore other techniques to create interest for the reader. Conclude with a transition or sentence leading into the body of your essay. Create interest or curiosity in your introductory paragraph to entice the reader to explore the body and conclusion of your essay.

Each paragraph in the body discusses the key points of your position. Start a new paragraph for each key point. Use detailed evidence, specific examples, concrete ideas, illustrations, statistics or other factual data to support your position. Details answer: **when, where, what, who, how far** and **how many.** Specific, concrete details have more strength than generalized or abstract statements. Use subordinate points to enhance your main points. Use your strongest point or detail as the climax of your essay.

The concluding paragraph summarizes your position, point of view, key points and recommendations. Did you use concrete details to unify or summarize your main points and make a final significant point? Your summary or conclusion should answer any questions generated in your introduction. Did your points and details convince the reader of your view or opinion with clarity, logical sequence and emotion? Did the audience learn something new about your topic? Does the research support your point of view or hypothesis? What would you like the reader to do? Did you compare, evaluate, explain or solve a problem? Make sure the essay answers your writing objective or purpose. You should not present a new topic in the conclusion. Does your essay generate new thought-provoking ideas for further discussion? Does it suggest solutions or action? End with a key quote to summarize your position. Remember, your concluding paragraph or paragraphs will stay in your reader's mind.

The title of your essay should express the specific topic, objective or purpose and attract the reader's attention. The title creates an interest for the reader to explore the introduction of your essay.

Before you write your essay, outline to organize and logically present your ideas. Write the draft, then revise and edit. Finally, proofread your essay for spelling, grammar and usage. You may need to rewrite your essay many times to generate your desired objective or purpose.

When writing an essay test, read the directions carefully. Underline key words in the question. Budget your time for outlining, drafting, revising, editing and proofreading. One strategy for your introductory paragraph is to convert the essay question into your essay thesis, specific topic or point of view, which will require the appropriate information to support your answer. Your outline should have a reasonable sequence, a natural order, which allows you to stay on your subject or thesis. Use bullets, numbers and headers to help your reader follow your writing. Review the writing style section of this book for ideas on how to write each sentence and paragraph.

Essay questions include recall, definition, narration, analysis, evaluation, persuasion and synthesis. Recall-type questions require you to present facts, most to least important, chronological order or to define key terms. A definition essay describes the whole by naming its parts, characteristics, origin, comparison or other key facts about the specific subject. In analytical essays, explain (exposition), classify, compare, contrast, show cause and effect, and conclude with your summary. In evaluation essays, state your opinion or judgment, then support your statements with data against some standard. Persuasive essays require you to convince your reader with key points backed by strong factual data. Synthesis essays require you to combine the above types of essays to form new ideas and concepts.

Ways to Present Your Information in an Essay

People remember most of what they learn first and last, so order of importance may provide the most effective tool for the reader to understand the writer's ideas.

Use the **increasing-order-of-importance strategy** by putting the least important idea first, then move to the next least important idea until you reach the most important idea, which leads your reader to the conclusion and important lasting impression. People tend to most easily remember the last idea. The **decreasing-order-of-importance strategy** starts with the most important point and ends with the least important point. This strategy creates immediate attention and strong initial impression. **Chronological-order-of-importance** takes the reader through a sequential order of steps for specific directions, events, processes or results.

Use the **general-to-specific format** by starting with a general statement and providing facts, evidence, statistics or other key information to support a specific statement.

Use the **specific-to-general format** by starting with specific details and conclude with a general statement.

Use the **sequential format** (step by step) to explain a process, describe a mechanism or provide instructions and procedures for a subject.

Use the **spatial format** to describe an object or a process according to the arrangement of the physical features. Describe a subject from top to bottom, from side to side, east to west, west to east, inside to outside, direction (up, down, north, south), shapes (rectangular, square, circle), proportion (one-third, one-half, two-thirds) or features described in relation to one another or the surroundings.

Use the **cause and effect strategy** to explain a specific occurrence. Show what cause created the effect. Each event may have multiple causes and multiple effects. Demonstrate that a cause or equally valid causes create an effect. The cause comes first, which leads to a result, the effect. Use consistent repetitive data, examples, illustrations or evidence to show the valid relationship. Incomplete evidence leads to false conclusions. One may not immediately observe remote causes; therefore, continue to test the cause-and-effect relationship. Another strategy is to express the effect first and then discuss the possible causes. Words used to indicate cause are **because of, since, created (by)**, and **caused (by)**. Words used to indicate effect are **since, hence, therefore, consequently**, and **as a result**. Cause tells us why something happened. Effect tells us what happened after a cause or a series of causes. Determine how causes are implied rather than stated. Ask yourself which cause or causes would logically create the effect. Given a particular event, determine the cause from observations and evidence. Predict the outcomes of actions or events. What effects can you predict will occur as a result of this event? An author will offer his or her opinion about the cause or effect of something rather than the facts. The reader must judge the validity of the author's analysis. Are the author's ideas logical? Does the author support the conclusion with valid data, facts or evidence?

Descriptive writing draws on all five senses—sight, touch, hearing, taste and smell—to help the reader form mental pictures of people, places, scenes, objects or understand the writer's point of view on the particular subject.

Help the reader visualize your ideas or bring your characters to life through emotions, strong feelings or imaginative comparisons such as figures of speech or metaphors.

Consider chronological order to describe incidents or events. Accurate presentation of details and concreteness help improve sensory impressions of your subject or point of view. Describe a person performing or demonstrating an action or process through the use of images and details. Describe different ways for the reader to understand your concepts through visual images. Describe in a natural order as you would observe the subject.

The **order of impression** outline starts with a descriptive fact that impresses you the most.

Definition Presentation Method

> Use dictionary definition
> Identify fundamental qualities/quantities and expand with additional details, examples, comparisons or other explanations
> Extend the definition by exploring additional qualities of your subject
> Understanding your reader's familiarity with a topic will help determine the language and vocabulary to use
> Use specific examples, graphs, charts and illustrations to help the reader understand the new subject
> Use an analogy to link the unfamiliar with a simpler or more familiar concept
> An analogy shows a resemblance in certain aspects between items normally unalike, which helps the reader to understand an unfamiliar term by showing its similarities with a more familiar subject
> Explain causes to help understand a particular subject
> Break the subject into its component parts
> Explore the origin of the subject or topic, especially when you want to explain why a word has a particular association
> Use a negative definition when the reader understands the subject contrasted

Visual Presentation in Essays

Use lists to name specific, comparable items, to break up complex statements or to emphasize key ideas. Provide an adequate transition before and after the list. When rank or sequence is unimportant, use bullets. Use words, phrases or short sentences with parallel structure. Use illustrations, photographs, tables, drawings, flow charts, organizational charts, graphs or maps to help the reader understand facts or ideas presented with simplicity, clarity, conciseness and directness. Use line, bar, pie and symbol graphs to present numerical data in a visual form. Label or caption your visual details and key identifying symbols, and show proportions or scales. Use consistent terminology and make sure the visual information connects with the text.

Analysis Methodologies

Analyze a topic or theme by:

> ➤ Classifying items into categories, classifications or divisions according to your specific purpose.

> ➤ Comparing all relevant characteristics or features of one item before you consider the next item; often used to weigh advantages and disadvantages of an item.

> ➤ Highlighting unique features when comparing similarities and differences of a particular item or point.

> ➤ Comparing and contrasting clearly evident items or a common category.

> ➤ Comparing the similarities of your subject first, then comparing the differences second.

> ➤ Comparing the same kind of items. (Imitation cowhide is almost as tough as real cowhide.)

> ➤ Comparing similarities and differences of the first major point before comparing the second major point.

When a double comparison occurs in the same sentence, complete the first comparison before you start the second. (The discovery of electricity was one of the great scientific discoveries in history, if not the greatest.)

Use **compare to** when establishing a general similarity. (Compared to the propeller air plane, a jet travels much faster.)

Use **compare with** to indicate a close examination of similarities or differences. (You **compared** the new movie **with** the old style of directing.)

Summarize your points in your conclusion.

Discuss one point completely before moving on to another major point.

Separate the whole into specific parts to understand your subject.

Review evidence, data, facts, then conclude with a summary.

Examine the causes that resulted in a particular consequence (cause and effect).

Why did something happen? Look for facts, details, evidence or clues that created the result.

Show how a new idea relates to information the reader already understands.

Break down the analyses into simple, comprehensible parts (paragraphs and sentences) and discuss them one by one in a logical order. Make sure each point contains appropriate language for the intended reader to thoroughly understand your particular point.

To show points of similarity, use transition words (**and, like, likewise, in the same, also, as, just as** or **both**).

To show differences, use transitions (**conversely, instead, rather, that, unlike, on the other hand, in contrast with, however, but, yet, on the contrary, nevertheless**).

The point-by-point method of comparing and contrasting starts with a topic sentence with a comparison. The remaining sentences in the paragraph identify examples of the comparison with a statement about *A*, then discuss a comparable fact of point *B*. Finally, conclude the paragraph with an important difference.

The block method of comparing and contrasting starts with all aspects of *A*, then with all aspects of *B*. The topic sentence describes the reason for the comparison. By comparing information, one can make an informed decision. Make sure the aspects of the two things that you analyze are comparable.

Process analysis gives directions, presents the steps in chronological order and defines all terms for a complete understanding of the process. Use transitional words such as **first, second, next, after, later** and **finally**. Summarize the benefits or uses of the particular process.

Exposition essays explain, expose, instruct or provide information about a specific topic for the reader. Start the essay with the main idea and add supporting facts, examples, illustrations or evidence to support your point of view. Each idea or point becomes a new paragraph. Use an appropriate order that will describe the mechanism, process or system. Use various order-of-importance strategies to answer the specific exposition essay.

A **persuasive essay** convinces the reader to agree with your position on a specific topic.

You must gain your audience's trust and confidence before they will agree with you.

Use key words and define crucial terms key to your argument or position.

Appeal to your reader through your competence, courtesy, emotions, ethical considerations and valid reasoning. Express your credentials and experience to help build trust and rapport with your readers. Create credibility and trust with valid points consistent with good morals and sense of right and wrong among your readers. Do not attack your opponent's argument with ridicule, but with your valid reasons. Do not turn the reader against you with sarcasm or crude remarks. To build your persuasive case, every paragraph, topic sentence and supporting sentence of your essay should provide supporting evidence of your view with relevant facts, details, examples, statistics, specific references, dates, quotes or expert opinions. Consider any possible conflicting opinions and incorporate your points to persuade your reader of your point of view. Do not wander from your main point of view. Avoid ambiguity and irrelevant or false claims. Use language that suits your purpose and your reader. Use few opinions. Use appropriate anecdote or history to create interest for the reader and lead into your topic. In your essay, use a combination of your persuasive logical reasoning, valid and logical points, emotion and ethics to promote your view to your reader.

There are two ways to persuade: appeal to the reader's sense of logic, or appeal to the reader's emotions. When writers rely only on appeals to emotion they neglect to provide any real evidence for why you should believe what they say. Sound, logical reasoning requires you to look beyond emotional appeals. Logic means using reason to form conclusions drawn from evidence and good common sense. Use emotional appeal to strengthen a logical argument. What reasons or evidence do you use to support your position? What reasons or evidence does the writer use to support their position? The introductory paragraph should catch your reader's attention with a concise statement of your position on a particular topic. Summarize the opposing view and then provide multiple points of your view. In the body or the middle paragraphs, discuss each of the valid points you made in the introductory paragraph. In the concluding paragraph, restate your argument and summarize why each of your valid points is stronger than the opposing view. Your points must show good intentions in the mind of the reader. What do you want to accomplish from your persuasive argument?

Do you want the reader to change their beliefs about your topic or have the reader take action? In your argument, consider appealing to your reader's reason or your reader's emotion. Add emotion to your point by appealing to your reader's physical, social or psychological needs. We all need food and water. We may desire freedom to do what we want. We desire power, belonging, fame or wealth. We also desire affection, love, security, high self-esteem and respect. Emotional appeal should not replace sound, logical reasoning nor stir up emotions that are dangerous or harmful.

Search for common ground. Get the reader to agree with one of your points and then the reader may agree with your other points. Project objections from your reader. To diffuse those objections, provide logical reasoning from your examples, facts, statistics or other forms of evidence in each of your points. Make sure every point is organized, unified and coherent. Do your research; check your facts, details, examples, quotes and evidence. You want to build trust and rapport, so do not lie.

Acknowledge your opponent's argument and counter each opposing point with your own convincing or stronger point. Use **however** to start your rebuttal. Do not give your opponent's points as much analysis or space as your points. Place your points last.

Another strategy is to show all opposing arguments, then counter with courteous, clear and concrete valid points.

In your argument, you should not:

- ➢ Misquote, falsely quote or quote an authority or expert who is in some other field
- ➢ Suppress or neglect evidence to favor your view
- ➢ Ignore opposing evidence
- ➢ Generalize from insufficient data or evidence
- ➢ Use a possibly false assumption as a reason to support your point of view
- ➢ Assume if *A* precedes *B*, then *A* must cause *B*, because of other probable reasons
- ➢ Shift from your topic to the opponent's
- ➢ Focus on the people or other unrelated issues, but focus on the issue(s)
- ➢ Use an analogy to define, because each item is specific and not a comparison
- ➢ Make a conclusion from an unrelated premise or false premise
- ➢ Lie or make deliberate misrepresentations
- ➢ Take the issue out of context with examples
- ➢ Discuss unrelated topics
- ➢ Present a limited number of possibilities if more exist
- ➢ Stereotype
- ➢ Offer the argument as proof
- ➢ Use ambiguity, confusing expressions, false claims or misleading questions
- ➢ Suggest your views are correct just because others believe your claim
- ➢ Build an argument on a fallacy

Narrative essay writing involves autobiographies, biographies, personal narratives or fictional stories in a form of short stories, poems, essays or novels through a series of events and characters. As the writer, define the purpose, audience, tone, objective or goal of the story (lessons learned) and then decide the best way to accomplish writing the story.

The story contains a plot, setting, characters and a theme or message that keeps the reader interested. State the theme or infer it from the dialogue, details of the plot, setting and characters. Concentrate on the story. Use dialogue, narration and events to move the story forward. As the writer, visualize what you want the reader to experience. Use specific, sensory (feel, look, smell, sound, taste) details that trigger your senses to create the desired images. Turn your thoughts into words so the reader feels they are part of the story.

The **plot**, a series of events with a beginning, middle and end, conveys your message. Consider plot event order to keep the reader's interest. Mysterious events or plot twists dramatically increase suspense for the reader. Find the appropriate pace to unfold the story.

The **setting** defines the time and place of events. The setting may represent a major character (nature or elements) in the story. If other characters challenge nature or attempt to conquer the elements, especially when the plot involves a dangerous place, then the setting becomes an important part of the story. Will the main characters survive their environment? Write directly about the setting; introduce the setting facts by using character dialogue, especially the narrator, or through the details of the story.

Introduce believable, memorable, realistic **characters** for the readers. Main characters have key roles; minor characters advance the plot. The protagonist represents the most important character and the antagonist represents the opposing or conflicting person or force (nature, society, mental). Avoid using names of real people, but try to find names that convey each major character's personality. Use as many characters (people, animals or other objects) to tell the story as possible. Reinforce character traits or reality through scenes, incidents or confrontations. Let the characters grow with the story. Develop the traits of the characters through their dialogues, thoughts and actions. The more the reader visualizes the characters, the more the reader will feel they know each character. Add physical descriptions (age, height, weight, eyes, hair, special attributes). Define background information that may affect a character's present behavior. Provide information on a character's personal data (ethnicity, hobbies, education, marital status, children, friends, family, pets, personality, image, education, religion and social class). Does a character have any particular traits (ambitious, bold, brave, cruel, dishonest, generous, gloomy, honest, humble, loving, loyal)? Add human spirit and nature, mannerisms or other factors to make each character more realistic. Establish goals for the characters; what do they want to accomplish? Instead of naming the characters' traits, let the reader reach their own interpretation through the characters' comments, thoughts and actions. Use the dialogue of the characters to further the plot. Would you rather read about some speaking and interacting, or read a narrative explanation? Identify each character by his or her dialogue without mentioning the speaker.

Develop **conflict** in the story by denying the characters from easily achieving their goals, fulfilling their needs or forcing the characters into a predicament. Let the characters struggle physically or mentally from outside or inside forces. The conflict engages the reader into the story; how will the main character overcome any obstacles? Use conflict to help you develop the characters. Many types of conflicts relate to food, water, health, physical safety, shelter, approval, esteem, friendship, love or nature. Other types of conflict the characters could battle include spiritual or philosophical conflict. Create suspense and tension as the characters face conflict until the story reaches its highest point, the **climax**.

Finally, the **climax** occurs followed by a logical resolution of any story conflicts or remaining issues.

Develop your narrative in different ways to create interest. Develop the narrative in a **chronological order**. Start the story at the end, then present events leading up to the end or begin the story in the middle and present events leading up to that point, and then finish the story. Use flash forwards or flash backs to enhance the story. Start your story with a setting and let the characters unfold. Start your story with a theme and allow the characters to experience life. Start with a plot and find characters as the story develops. Start with characters and let them interact as the plot develops. Start with a particular situation, then build characters into the story.

The writer develops a speaker, the personae, who tells the story from their point of view.

In the personal narrative, the first-person point of view tells the story. One of the characters narrates the story by describing the events, feelings and experiences of the story through that person's eyes. The **first-person** point of view establishes an intimacy and subjectivity between the writer and reader by expressing a personal view and perspective. Use personal pronouns (**I, we, you, they, us, we, our**). This person or character does not know the thoughts of the other characters. This point of view also gives the reader the sense that they are part of the story. **The third-person** point of view shifts focus from the writer to another person or thing to achieve objectivity. You want the subject to receive more emphasis than either you or the reader. The third-person point of view is unaffected by thoughts, feelings and expressions of the reader or writer and is generally not directly involved in the action.

In the **third-person (all knowing)** point of view, the narrator sees through the eyes of all the characters. Use pronouns, **he, she, they** or **it**. Write directly to the reader by use of the **second-person** pronoun, **you**. Use multiple characters to describe the story. Do not switch point of view during the story or confusion may occur. The author determines who speaks to the reader, the point of view, to create a relationship between the author, reader and characters in writing material.

HYPHEN (-)

Hyphenate:

- ➤ With a short line (-)
- ➤ A prefix creating a triple consonant
- ➤ A prefix ending with a vowel and root word starting with the same vowel (anti-intellectual, re-elect, re-enter)
- ➤ A word break at the end of line according to syllables
- ➤ Certain compound nouns (school-teacher) with equal value
- ➤ Compound numbers from twenty-one to ninety-nine
- ➤ Fractions written out (one-half, two-thirds, two-thirty-seconds)
- ➤ Prefixes before proper names such (anti-Semite, pro-Bush, pre-Sputnik)
- ➤ Words that end with the suffix elect (president-elect, commissioner-elect)
- ➤ Some words to avoid confusion (re-form, re-sent, re-cover, re-sign)
- ➤ Letters showing the spelling out a word (c-a-c-h-e)
- ➤ Prefixes and suffixes from the root or syllables (preempt, pre-empt)
- ➤ A letter or number modifier (10-cent, A-frame, A-bomb)

- Words used together (editor-in-chief, mother-in-law, runner-up)
- Multi-word compound nouns (five-year-old)
- To join numbers and adjectives (five-dollar profit, thirty-minute flight).
- A series of similar number-word adjectives. Do not repeat the term following the hyphen throughout the series. Add commas after the hyphens. (Bob scored baskets from ten-, fifteen-, and twenty feet. The first-, second-, and third-floor bathrooms needed new fixtures.)
- To write the time of day in words (eleven-thirty departure, five-fifteen in the morning).
- Two or more words functioning as a single adjective preceding the noun (ill-advised worker).
- After ex, great, self, half, all, post, pro or vice (all-American, pro-football, half-baked, half-an-hour, ex-professor, ex-President, self-reliant, Vice-President).
- When joining a prefix to a capitalized word (mid-Atlantic, trans-Siberian, un-American).
- Combine numbers with nouns (two-year term, fifty-cent fare, ten-year-olds, three-day-old fish)
- To form ethnic designations (African-American).
- To join a capital letter to a word (A-bomb, U-joint, T-Bird, U-boat)

Tie compound adjectives with a hyphen unless each of the words could modify the noun independently or the first word represents an adverb ending in **ly** (first-rate, out-of-date, twenty-five books, round orange plate, evenly coated paint, well-known).

Do not hyphenate the compound modifier that follows the modified term. (The calendar was out of date.)

Do not hyphenate words of one syllable (house, fire, wash).

Do not hyphenate so that a single letter stands alone (a-bort, fair-y, s-pare).

Divide hyphenated words at the hyphen.

Italics

Use italics to emphasize words, letters, figures, titles of books, musical works, movies, periodicals, paintings, magazines, newspapers, long plays or poems. Use underlining as an alternative to italics. Italicize names of planes, trains or ships unless naming the aircraft by model number (DC-10, Boeing 767). Emphasize foreign words with italics.

Jargon

Jargon represents unnecessary, inappropriate or inexact use of technical or specialized language.

Avoid technical terms for non-specialists unless the terms are defined first.

Properly used technical language communicates information clearly and concisely.

Know your audience when choosing specific words for your communication.

Metaphor

A metaphor, a figure of speech, compares two unlike things without using **like** or **as** (table leg, money tree).

A metaphor often helps clarify complex theories or objects by describing the less familiar term with the more familiar term.

A mixed metaphor (implied comparison) combines two or more incompatible comparisons (nose to the grindstone, keep your eye on the ball).

The verb matches the action and the subject of the metaphor.

Modifier

Modifiers—adverbs, adjectives, phrases or clauses—provide more information about the subject, verb or object of a clause.

Keep the modifier close to the pronoun or noun it describes. Do not confuse the reader by placing the modifier in an awkward position in the sentence, clause or phrase.

Verb phrases (gerund, infinitive, participle) should clearly and logically follow the modified item.

Use the modifier as a subordinate clause.

Put the subject and modifier in the same clause.

Place the adverb immediately before the intended modified word.

Nouns

Common nouns name nonspecific, abstract, concrete or collective persons, places, things, concepts, actions, qualities or objects. **Abstract nouns** refer to intangible items that do not appeal to the five senses (valor, peace, love, pride). **Concrete** nouns affect the five senses (shark, diamond). **Collective nouns**, plural in meaning but singular in form with a singular verb or pronoun, describe a group of people, things, places, concepts, actions or qualities (audience, crowd, family, data, staff, army, athletics, civics, committee, crowd, ethics, family, majority, mathematics, news, physics, team). Nouns can function as subjects of verbs, objects of verbs, objects of prepositions, subjective complements, adjectives, adverbs or appositives. Use a plural verb or pronoun with collective nouns within a group (pants, pincers, scissors, wages). **Proper nouns** name a specific person, place, thing, concept, action, quality or object which begins with an uppercase letter (Henry). **Compound nouns** name two or more nouns or two words joined by a hyphen that function as a single noun. Items uncountable, something one cannot separate, represent **mass nouns** (oil, gas, gold, coffee, electricity). Do not use the articles **a** or **an** with these nouns. Items countable represent singular or plural nouns you can count (one book, fifty-two cards). Use the articles **a** or **an** with a singular **count noun** but not with the plural count noun (an apple, a basket, some bananas, any cherries). To create possession for a singular noun or plural noun not ending in **s**, add an apostrophe and an **s**. To create possession for a plural noun ending in **s,** add an apostrophe to the **s**. To show joint possession with coordinate nouns, use the possessive with the last noun (Jack and Jill's water pail). To show individual possession with coordinate nouns, use possession for each noun (Jack's and Jill's water pails). Add **'s** to living things and use the **of** phrase with inanimate objects to form possession (side of the barn).

If the singular noun ends in **s**, just add the apostrophe after the **s**.

In a multiword term, add **'s** to the last word (father-in-law's).

Use **'s** with time expressions (today's, week's, Friday's).

To make a noun plural:

- ➢ Add an **s**
- ➢ Add **es** if the noun ends in **s, sh, ch** or **x**
- ➢ If the noun ends in a consonant and **y**, change **y** to **i** and add **es** (city to cities)
- ➢ If the noun ends in a vowel and **y**, add **s** (key to keys)
- ➢ If the noun ends in **uy**, change **y** to **ies**
- ➢ Add **s** to most nouns ending in **f** except some examples change **f** to **ves** (self to selves or wolf to wolves)
- ➢ Do not change **f** to **ves** for specific names (Wolfs Book)
- ➢ In compound words, make the main word plural (mother-in-law to mothers-in-law, mixup to mixups, takeoff to takeoffs)
- ➢ Compound words ending in **ful**, add an **s**
- ➢ For other nouns, change their spelling (child to children, foot to feet, mouse to mice, man to men, goose to geese, tooth to teeth and woman to women)
- ➢ Some nouns stay the same for plural (deer, sheep, series and moose)

Nationalities ending in **ese** have the same singular and plural form (Portuguese).

To form most plural nouns, add an **s** (auto to autos, book to books, car to cars, computer to computers, piano to pianos, skill to skills, soprano to sopranos, tobacco to tobaccos).

Add **es** to make plural most nouns ending in **ch, s, sh, ss, x** or **z** (boxes, brushes, buzzes, churches, dishes, dresses, guesses, indexes, kisses, lunches, waltzes).

Some nouns add **en** to form the plural (child to children, man to men, ox to oxen, woman to women).

Some nouns require word changes (foot to feet, goose to geese, louse to lice, mouse to mice, tooth to teeth).

For nouns ending in **y** preceded by a consonant, change the **y** to **i** and add **es** (fly to flies, enemy to enemies, lady to ladies, rally to rallies, sky to skies, study to studies).

For nouns ending in **y** preceded by a vowel, add **s** (monkey to monkeys, turkey to turkeys, alley to alleys, key to keys, play to plays).

Some nouns ending in **f** or **fe** form the plural by changing the **f** or **fe** to **ves**; others just add **s** (beliefs, calf to calves, chiefs, cuffs, elf to elves, gulf to gulfs, half to halves, kerchiefs, knife to knives, leaf to leaves, loaf to loaves, proofs, self to selves, shelf to shelves, thief to thieves, wife to wives, wolf to wolves).

For some words ending in **o** add **es** to the singular noun (domino to dominoes, embargo to embargoes, echo to echoes, hero to heroes, potato to potatoes, tomato to tomatoes, veto to vetoes).

To those words that end in a vowel followed by an **o**, add **s** to form their plural (patios, radios, studios, videos).

When the final **o** follows a consonant, some words add **s**, while others use **es** (albinos, altos, banjos, broncos, logos, silos, sopranos, bravo to bravos or bravoes, buffalo to buffalos or buffaloes, zero to zeros or zeroes, cargo to cargos or cargoes).

Add apostrophe **s** to form plurals of letters, figures, signs, words or phrases (m's or 9's).

In certain hyphenated words, only the most important part of the word forms the plural (editors-in-chief, mothers-in-law).

Some plurals of titles are changed like this: Mr. to Messers., Miss to Misses, Master to Masters); there is no plural for Mrs.

Some words written as plurals ending in **ics** usually have a singular verb (ethics, athletics, mathematics, electronics, economics, politics, physics).

Some words written as plurals represent a plural noun (clothes, thanks, billiards, suds, shears, goods).

Some words can represent a plural or singular form (cattle, sheep, deer, gross, salmon, trout, fish, grouse).

Change Latin singular words ending in **um** to **a,** or ending in **us** to **i** (alumnus to alumni, bacteria to bacterium, curriculum to curricula, datum to data, fungus to fungi, medium to media, stratum to strata).

Change Greek singular words ending in **sis** to **ses** or **xis** to **xes** (analysis to analyses, axis to axes, basis to bases, oasis to oases, parenthesis to parentheses, thesis to theses).

A subjective complement gives information about the subject. (A dolphin is a mammal.)

An **appositive**, a noun or noun phrase, follows and enhances another noun or noun phrase. (Mark Twain, **an 18th century author**, wrote Huckleberry Finn.)

With a noun form used as a **predicate nominative**, the noun follows a linking verb and renames the subject. (She is my doctor, noun form. His reason for not attending school: he hurt his leg, noun clause.)

Novel or Story

Answer each of these questions to structure your novel. See narrative essay writing.

- ➢ Who, characters
- ➢ What, conflict
- ➢ When, time
- ➢ Where, place
- ➢ Why, characters' motivations
- ➢ How, resolve the conflict
- ➢ Do you have a protagonist and an antagonist?
- ➢ Have you established the time and place for the action?
- ➢ Have you structured your story with a clear beginning, middle and end?
- ➢ Is the conflict resolved in a logical way?
- ➢ Have you identified your audience?
- ➢ Did you show, not tell, by using description?
- ➢ Did you create a tantalizing title?
- ➢ Did you revise and edit your work?

Objects

An **object** represents a complement, one or more nouns, pronouns, adjectives or a nominative element that receives, is affected by or is the result of the action of the verb and completes the meaning of the subject and verb.

The **direct object** positioned after an action verb answers the question **what** or **whom** about the verb and subject.

Do not make an object of the verb part of a prepositional phrase.

Certain **transitive verbs** (*give, wish, cause, tell* and their synonyms or antonyms) require a direct object to complete their meaning.

Use the objective case for personal pronouns representing objects.

The **indirect object** of the verb represented by a noun, pronoun or nominative element precedes the direct object and answers the question **to whom** or **for whom** the action of the verb impacted.

An **object of a preposition** answers the question **whom** or **what** after the preposition. (Give that book **to me**.)

A noun, pronoun or nominative element represents the **object of a verbal phrase** such as a gerund, participle or infinitive.

Objects can be compound (between you and me).

An **object complement**, a noun or an adjective, completes the meaning of a direct object. (They elected Eric **president**. You made her **angry**.)

PARAGRAPH

A **paragraph** consists of a topic sentence and a sequence of sentences that support, unify and develop the topic sentence. The **topic sentence** states the purpose, major point or main idea of the paragraph. If the topic sentence begins the first sentence in the paragraph, your reader can focus on the supporting details throughout the paragraph.

If the topic sentence starts in the middle of the paragraph, you can provide supporting details before you actually state the topic sentence. Providing details first can help to decrease resistance to your main idea, especially if you think your audience will disagree with your topic. Try to include the same number of facts or details above and below the topic sentence; this will provide a stronger case for your main idea of the paragraph.

By placing the topic sentence last in a paragraph, you create suspense or even a dramatic effect. A topic sentence at the end of a paragraph also serves as a summary or conclusion of the previous detailed sentences. Advertisements and persuasive writing use the end of the paragraph topic sentences effectively. To draw your readers into the paragraph, create sentences that imply a topic sentence. Use the context of the paragraph or paragraphs to help you understand an implied topic sentence. Provide a series of clues through structure and language to get the main idea across. Finding an implied main idea requires you to connect the ideas in the paragraph or the passage. Use implications to convey meaning rather than directly stating the author's ideas. Readers prefer suggestion to direct statements.

Each sentence in a paragraph should expand the topic sentence by providing supporting facts, opinions, details (people, events), statistics, illustrations, definitions or examples.

Supporting sentences explain your ideas, beliefs or reasons for an action, justify your statements, provide proof, describe, narrate, analyze, evaluate, synthesize or provide details emphasizing your topic sentence. Create a strong impact by stating your strongest reason or detail last. Include enough sentences to provide a logical development of your topic sentence. Every sentence in the paragraph should contribute to the development of the main idea of the paragraph by providing unity and cohesion.

The **concluding sentence** may restate the main idea, give your opinion, state a decision, call for action or summarize previous statements or the point of your paragraph. You should not introduce new ideas in the concluding sentence or attempt to rewrite your topic sentence. Use transitional words, phrases or clauses to end the paragraph and proceed to the next paragraph. If a transitional sentence starts a paragraph, follow with the topic sentence. Use transitional words of sequence, contrast, comparison, concession, example, consequence, restatement, time or conclusion to achieve a smooth flow of ideas that relate one paragraph to another. Transitional words of sequence, likeness or addition include **again, and, finally, first, furthermore, in addition, likewise, meanwhile, moreover, next, second, similarity** and **third**. Transitional words of emphasis include **chiefly, equally, even more important, indeed** and **moreover**. Transitional words of contrast, compare or concession include **but, on the contrary, on the other hand, of course, however, still, no doubt, nevertheless, granted that, similarly, likewise, also, nevertheless, conversely, although, yet** and **admittedly**. Transitional words of example include **for example, for instance, as an example, specifically, consider as an illustration, that is** and **such as**. Transitional words of consequence or cause and effect include **thus, so, then, it follows, as a result, therefore** and **hence**. Transitional words of restatement include **in short, that is, in effect** and **in other words.** Transitional words of time include **afterward, next, then, as soon as, later, until, when, finally, last** and **at last**. Transitional words of conclusion include **finally, therefore, thus** and **to sum up**. For effective writing, do not start every sentence with a transition. One technique is to start the first sentence of each new paragraph with a transition phrase combined with a clause or words with a topic sentence.

Start a new paragraph with each new idea. Connect each new paragraph with a connective word, phrase or sentence that refers to a word or sentence in the previous paragraph. Use details, key words or phrases from the previous paragraph to advance your major point or topic. Appropriate conjunctions and transition words help tie ideas from one paragraph to the next. Use the first sentence of a paragraph to connect ideas between two paragraphs. Use parallel structure by repeating the pattern of a phrase or clause in the previous paragraph. Use enumeration: **first, second, third** and **finally**. Use an opening sentence that summarizes the preceding paragraph, then develop the rest of the paragraph with a new idea or continue to develop previous ideas. Ask a question at the end of one paragraph and answer it at the beginning of the next.

A start or change of dialogue starts a new paragraph.

Transitional paragraphs, which may not have topic sentences, establish connections with your main idea, introductory, middle and ending paragraphs. End your paragraph in an appropriate tone for the specific purpose and reader. Short paragraphs increase the pace of your writing and long paragraphs decrease the pace of your writing.

PARALLEL STRUCTURE

Parallel structure repeats words, phrases, clauses and even sentences with the same grammatical structure or form with equal rank (equality of ideas) to create rhythm, emphasis, balance, impact, crispness, clarity, smoothness and conciseness.

Parallel constructions relate closely in thought, in length and in construction, which balances one another.

Create tension by leaving out conjunctions.

Overuse of parallelism creates wordiness.

Grammatical repetition creates emphasis and memorable phrases.

Examples:

- ➤ "The best of times and worst of times" repeats an adjective, preposition and noun.
- ➤ In the Gettysburg Address: We cannot dedicate, we cannot consecrate, we cannot hallow this ground.
- ➤ By their size, by their volume, by their weight

Use parallel construction for comparing and contrasting ideas.

Each element in a series should have a similar form and structure. Each phrase or clause in a list should begin with the same part of speech (a preposition, an article, a pronoun, a subordinating conjunction, a helping verb or an infinitive). If you make a statement about two subjects, follow with a statement about the first subject and complete the thought with a balancing statement of the other subject. Correlative conjunctions (**either ... or, neither ... nor, not only ... but also**) require parallel structure.

PARENTHESES ( )

Parentheses enclose words, phrases and sentences that add, supplement or clarify a statement or information without altering the meaning of the sentence. Parentheses represent a nonessential modifier in a sentence. A comma following a parenthetical word, phrase or clause appears outside the closing parenthesis. In some footnote forms, parentheses enclose the publisher, place of publication and date of publication: Kingston, George, *Exciting Adventures of Hydra and Muste Otter* (Los Gatos: G Sharp Productions, 2001), p. 50. Parentheses enclose numbers, figures, letters or dates, which indicate sequence or division (1), (2), (a), (b) or (1999). A complete sentence within parentheses requires ending punctuation, which should be inside the closing parenthesis.

Phrase

A **phrase,** a group of related words, functions in a sentence as a single part of speech (adjective, adverb, noun or verb), but not as an independent and complete thought.

A phrase adds detail, variety, emphasis and expands ideas or improves the precise meaning of a sentence.

A **prepositional phrase** starts with a preposition plus other words (modifiers), and ends with an object of the preposition (noun or pronoun). Use a prepositional phrase as an adjective or adverb, which answers the question **which one** or **what kind**. Position the prepositional phrase near the noun or pronoun. Prepositional phrases strengthen spatial relationships with words such as **above, at, below, in around, into, near, of** or **over**. Use coordinating conjunctions to connect two or more prepositional phrases.

An **adverb prepositional phrase** describes or modifies an adjective, adverb or verb, and asks where, when, in what manner or to what extent.

An **appositive phrase** renames a noun or pronoun and is usually placed directly after the noun or pronoun it modifies. Use an appositive phrase once you define or name the specific noun or pronoun. Use commas to establish the meaning of nonessential (nonrestrictive) appositives but not essential appositives. Connect compound appositives with correlative conjunctions such as **and, but, or, for, nor** or **yet**.

With a **verbal phrase**, which includes gerund, infinitive and participle phrases, use the verb form as another part of speech, but not as a verb. Verb phrases can have a subject or take an object.

Adverbs or **adverbial phrases** describe verb phrases.

A **participle phrase**, a verbal phrase consisting of a participle and object, a complement (if any) or modifiers, functions as an adjective with the present participle ending in **ing** and with the past participles usually ending in **ed, t,** or **en** (working quickly, jumped, burnt, spoken, going to the movies, caught in a rush, or having driven to the country).

Participles do not precede a helping verb. Do not confuse participles and verbs.

Use the perfect participle of the verb to form the participle phrase too.

Place a participle phrase before or after the word it describes. If the phrase describes the word that follows, then separate the phrase with commas. Make sure the participle phrase modifies the correct noun or pronoun.

Form a **gerund phrase**, a verbal phrase, by adding **ing** to the nonfinite verb form and any objects or modifiers. A gerund phrase can function as a noun, subject, direct object, indirect object, object of a preposition, predicate nominative, subjective complement or appositive (walking, eating, fighting or seeing is believing). When using a gerund phrase to start a sentence, do not forget to put yourself or the subject into the main sentence. Only the possessive form of a noun or pronoun should precede a gerund. Some verbs require a gerund when used as a direct object: **acknowledge, anticipate, advise, avoid, admit, appreciate, delay, dislike, discuss, evade, enjoy, escape, finish, include, insist on, image, keep on, mention, mind, object to, postpone, practice, put off, quiet, recall, recommend, regret, resent, resist, risk, support, talk about, tolerate, understand.**

Form an **infinitive phrase**, another verbal phrase, by adding **to** to the verb with objects and modifiers to act as a noun, adjective or adverb. If using **to be,** then the subject of the infinitive takes the objective case. Form a **split infinitive** by placing an adverb or adverbial phrase between **to** and the verb. Verbs that follow an infinitive: **afford, care, claim, consent, decide, decline, demand, deserve, expect, fail, give, hesitate, hope, intend, manage, mean, offer, permission, plan, prepare, promise, pretend, refuse, seem, struggle, tend, threatened, volunteer, vote, wait, want.**

Prepositions

Prepositions link a noun, pronoun or object to another word or words in the sentence.

Prepositions: **about, aboard, above, according to, across, after, against, along, amid, among, amongst, around, astride, as, at, athwart, because, before, behind, beneath, besides, between, beyond, besides, but, by, considering, concerning, despite, dispute, down, during, except, from, for, inside, in, in place of, into, less, like, midst, minus, near, notwithstanding, of, off, on, onto, out, outside, opposite, over, past, regarding, since, through, throughout, to, toward, under, until, underneath, up, upon, via, wanting, with, within** and **without**.

Use **like** or **as** as a preposition to join a noun.

Do not use **like** or **as** as a conjunction to introduce an adverb clause. Only conjunctions and relative pronouns introduce clauses. Avoid the use of **like** for **as** or **as if**.

Generally, avoid ending a sentence with a preposition, unless it falls naturally.

Avoid using redundant prepositions: **off of, in back of, inside of, at about**. Use either **at** or **about**.

Pronouns

A pronoun, a person or persons speaking, spoken to, spoken of or thing spoken of, replace a noun (antecedent) or another pronoun to avoid noun repetition. Pronouns agree with the antecedent in person, gender and number. Place a pronoun close to its antecedent to reduce confusion. The nominative (subjective), objective and possessive cases represent the various forms of a pronoun that show how it relates to other words in the sentence.

The **subjective case** represents a person or thing acting or a pronoun acting as the subject of the clause or sentence (I, we, he, she, it, you, they, who). The **objective case** indicates the person or thing acted upon, especially when used as the object of the verb or a preposition (me, us, him, her, it, you, them, whom). For example, John scared Tom and me (me, object of verb). Another example: Between you and me, John did not help us (me, object of the preposition). The **possessive case** represents the person or thing owning or possessing (my, mine, our, ours, his, her, its, your, yours, their, whose). **Any, each, few, most, have** and **some** form possession only in **of phrases** (the facts of each case); otherwise, use an apostrophe (anybody's).

Linking verbs connect a pronoun (subjective case) to its antecedent even when the pronoun follows the verb (subjective complement). (He is the treasurer of the organization. The treasurer of the organization is he.)

Personal pronouns consist of:

First person represents the speaker.

> First person singular: **I, me, mine, my**
> First person plural: **we, us, our, ours**

Second person represents the person spoken to.

> Second person singular: **you, your, yours, thou, thee, thy, thine**
> Second person plural: **you, your, yours**

Third person represents the one spoken about.

> Third person singular: **he, him, his, she, her, hers, it, its, whom**
> Third person plural: **they, them, their, theirs, its, whose**

The English language does not have third person singular pronouns that refer to one person either male or female. No singular person refers to both sexes. If you need a pronoun to refer to words like **anyone, anybody, everybody, somebody, everyone** or **someone**, use **he, she, his** or **her**.

Nominative (subjective) case pronouns substitute the subject, noun, verb form **to be** or the predicate nominative that performs the action. Use subjective case if the pronoun precedes the verb.

Objective (accusative) case pronouns that receive the action substitute for a direct object, indirect object, object of the preposition (between you and me) or subject of an infinitive.

Use objective case for pronouns following action verbs or gerunds. (The company hired me. Seeing Mary for the first time meant everything to him.) If the pronoun follows the verb, use the objective case.

Use the **possessive case** to show ownership (**my, mine, your, yours, his, its, our, ours, their, theirs, whose** and **whoever**). Do not confuse possessive pronouns and contractions such as **its** with **it's**, **your** with **you're**, **their** with **they're**, **whose** with **who's**.

	Subjective case	Objective case	Possessive case
First Person Singular	I	me	my, mine
First Person Plural	we	us	our, ours
Second Person Singular	you	you	your, yours
Second Person Plural	you	you	your, yours
Third Person Singular	he	him	his
Third Person Singular	she	her	her, hers
Third Person Singular	it	it	its
Third Person Plural	they	them	their, theirs
Singular relative pronouns	who, whoever	whom, whomever	whose
Plural relative pronouns	whoever	whomever	whosoever

Reflexive pronouns refer back to a noun or pronoun that ends in **self** or **selves** (**yourself, yourselves, myself, herself, itself, oneself, ourselves, himself** or **themselves**). Avoid substituting the reflexive pronouns **myself** for **I** or **me** and **ourselves** for **we** or **us**. Use a reflexive pronoun when the subject and object are the same.

Demonstrative pronouns direct attention to a specific person, place or thing (**this, that, these** and **those**). Identify demonstrative pronouns from a clear antecedent. (Those cats ate the fish.)

Relative pronouns begin a subordinate clause with **that, which, who, whom** and **whose**.

The relative pronoun, either singular or plural, separates into the nominative (subject) case, objective case and possessive (ownership) case. The relative pronoun connects and establishes the relationship between a dependent clause and main (independent) clause. Use **that** with a restrictive clause, a clause that is essential to the meaning of a sentence. Use **which** with a nonrestrictive clause, a clause that adds information and that is set off by commas but is unnecessary for sentence completion. **Which** should refer to the preceding words in a sentence. **That** or **which** refers to things, groups and unnamed animals. If the antecedent consists of a group of words, place the relative pronoun at the end of the group. Use **who** or **whoever** when the pronoun represents the subject of a verb or predicate nominative. Substitute the personal pronoun **he** or **they** in your sentence; if yes, use **who**. If **him** or **them** fits the sentence, then use **whom**. Use **whom** or **whomever** when the pronoun represents the direct object of a verb or the object of a preposition. (Whom are you calling? You are calling whom? These are direct objects. Whom are you talking to? Whom is the object of the preposition **to**.)

Reciprocal pronouns (one another, each other) indicate the relationship of one item to another. Use **each other** when referring to two people or things. Use **one another** when referring to more than two people or things. (They played well with each other. The basketball players played well with one another.) Place a noun in apposition between the antecedent and relative pronoun.

Interrogative pronouns ask a question, such as **what, which, who, whom** or **whose**.

Indefinite pronouns do not name specific people, places, objects or things but specify a class or group of people or things (another, anyone, anything, both, each, everybody, some, several, all, any, few, many).

Match singular pronouns with singular verbs (another, anyone, anybody, each, everyone, everybody, everything, either, little, much, nobody, nothing, neither, no one, one, other, somebody, someone or something). Match plural pronouns with plural verbs (**both, few**;

others, several). Some pronouns represent singular or plural nouns or pronouns (all, any, more, most, none, some). A pronoun should clearly refer to a specific antecedent. First and second personal pronouns do not normally require an antecedent (I like my house). Use the noun first before using the pronoun to prevent confusion. Match multiple pronouns to the specific antecedent. Repeat the noun from the previous paragraph before substituting a pronoun. To add a possessive quality to a noun, change that noun into an adjective and not an antecedent. Use the pronouns **it, this** or **which** to refer to an antecedent. Generally, avoid using a pronoun to refer to the title of a document in the document's first sentence.

QUOTATIONS MARKS (" ")

Quotation marks enclose a direct quotation, a speaker's exact words. Identify the speaker at the beginning, middle or end of the quote. Use commas to separate the speaker and the quote. When the speaker's name follows the quote, use a comma, then closing quote marks to end the quote, and then a period at the end of the sentence after the speaker. ("I like to eat fish," said Bob.) Put periods, commas, question marks or exclamation marks inside the ending quotation marks if the end marks are part of the quote. Put colons, semicolons, dashes and footnote numbers outside of the closing quotation marks. If a question mark or exclamation point would normally occur in the quote, then use that end mark, then closing quote marks and finally a period at the end of the sentence after the speaker. ("Do you like to eat fish?" asked Carol. "I like to eat all kinds of fish!" yelped Bob.) When the speaker's name precedes the quote, place a comma, then insert open quotation marks and finally the appropriate end mark, then closing quotation marks. (Carol said, "I like to eat fish." Carol asked, "Do you like to eat fish?" Bob yelped, "I like to eat fish!")

Use a colon to separate quoted material.

Any material you add as a clarifying comment should be put in square brackets.

[Sic] represents the quote exactly as it appeared in the original source even if the quote suggests obvious errors.

Capitalize the first letter of the first word of a direct quotation.

Do not capitalize the first word of an interrupted quotation unless the second section of the quote begins a new sentence or uses a proper noun. Notice the comma and closing quotation marks before **said** and the comma after the speaker, then the opening quotation marks to finish the quote followed by the appropriate end mark and closing quotation marks. ("Everybody enjoyed the ice cream," said Amy, "except for Tim." "Everyone enjoyed the ice cream," said Amy. "The French vanilla tasted the best among the party.")

Put a period after the named speaker.

Use single quotation marks to enclose quoted material or the titles of short works within a quotation enclosed by double quotation marks.

Put a period before final quotation marks.

Do not use quotation marks for indirect quotations or paraphrases.

Indent ten spaces (five spaces more than a regular indent) from the left margin and block direct quotations longer than four typed lines.

Triple space before and after a quotation for three or more lines of verse or five or more lines of prose and single-space the quotation.

If you quote consecutive paragraphs, put quotation marks at the beginning of each paragraph but only at the end of the last paragraph.

Use quotation marks to indicate the title of a painting, statue, essay, chapter, short stories, poems, written material less than twenty pages, songs, magazine articles, chapter titles, television programs, holy books, legislative documents and radio episode titles. Underline or italicize titles of books and periodicals.

Do not introduce a long quote into a sentence because of possible difficulty in following the completed sentence.

Use quotation marks to identify phrases, words or sentences that need special consideration (**"rule of thumb," "accept as except"**).

Use quotation marks to set off a definition.

Use ellipses (three spaced periods) to indicate that you have cut part of quotation material within a sentence. When missing the beginning quoted material, start the quote without a capital letter and without ellipses. If a sentence ends with ellipses, add one more dot for the period. "John decided not to play baseball with the ... players. ..."

Ask yourself: Will the quote or paraphrase help you obtain your writing goal?

Use quotes word for word only where your source concisely states information to help develop your topic.

Start a new paragraph for each change of speaker.

Dialogue allows you to naturally tell your story. Use dialogue to converse with the reader.

Do not put quotation marks in a series of uninterrupted sentences of one speaker. Instead put quotation marks at the beginning of the quoted paragraph and quotation marks at the end of the paragraph.

Use quotation marks as ditto marks instead of repeating a line of words or numbers directly beneath an identical set.

A is the difference between B and C.
B " "   "   "   D and E.
C " "   "   "   F and G.

Use quotation marks to give credit in a footnote of accurate original material.

REDUNDANCY

Redundancy represents unnecessary repetition of words, phrases and ideas to convey your intended meaning.

Make every word count by writing simply and directly to the point.

Omit unnecessary words, phrases, clauses or sentences.

Use important details.

Turn phrases into verbs or fewer words.

Combine related sentences to achieve clarity.

Revise sentences that begin with expletives (**it is, there is**, and **there are**) with an action verb.

Make passive sentences active.

Cut buzz words or phrases which do not add meaning to the sentence.

Use specific, concrete language to stimulate the senses.

Use commas and pronouns to reduce unnecessary words.

Repetition

Repetition uses the same sound, word, phrase, line or grammatical structure over and over.

Use repetition to link related ideas, create rhythm, build a sustained effect, show importance and emphasize key points.

For example, Lincoln wrote in his Gettysburg speech, "We cannot dedicate, we cannot consecrate, we cannot hallow this ground."

Repetition and parallelism add to the style of the writer.

Do not repeat words with different meanings.

Avoid repetitions of awkward sounds (emphony).

Repeat key words from a previous sentence or paragraph to achieve transition.

Revise

Once you write your material, revise for conciseness, coherence and unity; make it simple, direct and to the point. Ways to revise your writing:

- ➢ Turn a subordinate clause into a prepositional phrase
- ➢ Leave out relative pronouns
- ➢ Convert clauses into phrases
- ➢ Convert sentences to phrases (infinitive)
- ➢ Convert phrases to single words
- ➢ Combine related sentences or sentences that repeat or are redundant
- ➢ Omit unnecessary details or ideas that do not add to your point of view or intended thoughts for your reader
- ➢ Eliminate unnecessary adjectives, adverbs or other words that do not add meaning to your writing
- ➢ The fewer words used, the more efficiently and pleasurably the reader can grasp your ideas
- ➢ Use prepositions, infinitives or participles to shorten sentences
- ➢ Convert adjectives into nouns with endings of **y, like, ful, less, ly, able, ed, ing, ness, ment, ion, ize, fy, izement, fication**
- ➢ Avoid nouns or adjectives created from verbs; instead of *reach an agreement* use **agree**, or instead of *make an objection* use **object**
- ➢ Use prefixes to shorten phrases (*before one could finish it* use *unfinished*, instead of *I had written over again*, use *rewritten*, instead of *spelled wrongly* use *misspelled*)
- ➢ Convert verbs into nouns using **ing**, a gerund or verb noun (*like to dance—dancing*)
- ➢ Stay away from clichés and pretentious phrases
- ➢ Use **ed** and **ing** to form participles from verbs
- ➢ Convert verbs into adjectives by using **ed, able** or **ing** (*that warmed our hearts—heart warming*)
- ➢ Use **like, ful** or **less** to shorten words (*like a lady—ladylike, full of joy—joyful, that has no point—pointless*)
- ➢ Change words ending with **ive** (adjective) and **tion** (noun) into verbs (*creative* to *create, examination* to *examine*)
- ➢ Substitute **to be, to have** and **to make** verbs

- ➤ Turn nouns into verbs
- ➤ Turn clauses or phrases into adjectives by taking the most important word in the clause or phrase and adding **y** (*that is in the shade—shady*)

After you revise your writing, read it aloud.

Do not leave out words if it may cause confusion or doubt for the reader.

Do not leave out a pronoun for a substituted noun.

Make sure each sentence has a subject and a predicate.

Review sentence variety using simple, compound and complex constructions for intended meaning and readable content.

Design your sentence structure to reflect your thoughts for the reader.

Arrange sentences to create emphasis and indicate the direction of your thoughts.

Ideas should relate with a logical order and a clear transition between ideas, sentences or paragraphs. The reader should move smoothly from one relative point to another. Use your outline to stay on point; do not stray onto side issues.

Put the main idea in a main or independent clause.

Put less important information in subordinate clauses.

For equal ideas, use sentence structure to reflect equal importance.

Are your sentences too short or too long?

Rewrite a sentence if a misplaced adverb or modifying phrase creates confusion for the reader.

Will the position of a paragraph, sentence, clause, phrase or word increase or decrease the emphasis on your particular thought?

Avoid emphasis of anticlimaxes.

Avoid weak qualifiers buried in the middle of a sentence (**in my opinion**, **it seems to me** or **in general**).

Does each sentence in a paragraph support or clarify the topic sentence?

Does the topic sentence define the purpose of the paragraph?

Does each paragraph support the main theme of your writing?

Do not combine words that change your intended meaning.

Do not leave out commas, especially to show where the main clause starts.

Does each word add to the sentence?

Revision Checklist:

- ➤ Clear purpose
- ➤ Language and topic suited to your audience
- ➤ Organized in a logical way
- ➤ Concise and correct sentences
- ➤ Fluid and graceful writing
- ➤ Exact words for specific meaning
- ➤ Entertaining and fun to read
- ➤ Free of biased language
- ➤ Corrected grammar, usage, spelling, punctuation and capitalization

SEMICOLON (;)

A semicolon connects related ideas representing a strong comma or a shorter stop than the period. Substitute a semicolon for a coordinating conjunction between two independent clauses. (I like to eat fish on Fridays; I also eat chicken on Wednesdays.) Use a semicolon between a main clause and a conjunctive adverb (**accordingly, besides, consequently, for example, furthermore, hence, however, if, inside, moreover, nevertheless, otherwise, therefore, thus**) and place a comma after the conjunctive adverb. (I will not finish today; moreover, I doubt that I will finish this week.) The conjunctive adverb, **moreover**, belongs to the second clause.

95

Use a semicolon to separate items in a series that contain internal commas (old, comfortable jeans; rugged, warm sweaters).

Do not use a semicolon to separate a dependent clause from an independent clause; use a comma or a subordinating conjunction.

Place a semicolon outside closing quotation marks because it is not part of the quote.

Use a semicolon instead of a connecting word when two titles and statements are closely related in thought.

Do not use a semicolon to enclose a parenthetical element that contains commas; use parentheses or dashes.

Do not use a semicolon as a mark of anticipation or enumeration; use a colon.

Sentence

A **sentence** consists of a group of words with a subject and a predicate that expresses a complete thought with an end mark (period, question mark, exclamation point); it is where one idea ends and the next begins.

A **subject** answers the question who, whom or what (nouns or pronouns) in the sentence.

Here or **there** do not function as the subject of a sentence.

A **predicate** describes something about the subject—what the subject does, did or what the subject is with a verb as a base and possible verb modifiers and complements to complete the thought. The predicate nominative (noun) and predicate adjective (adjective), also known as a subjective complement, represent a noun or adjective in the predicate of a sentence, which completes the meaning of a linking verb by describing or renaming the subject of the verb.

Verbs without action generally require a linking verb. In a question, a verb often comes before the subject. A sentence may have more than one verb, resulting in compound verbs.

Instead of using two sentences relating to the same person or thing or using a double predicate in a sentence, combine sentences or separate verbs by forming an independent clause and dependent clause with **who** or **which**. Verbs usually appear close to the subject to prevent confusion.

Command sentences usually omit the subject.

One usually writes dialogue as fragments or incomplete sentences because people do not normally speak in complete sentences.

A **simple sentence** consists of one or more subjects, verbs (compound), adjectives, or adverbs, but it has only one independent clause and no subordinate clauses.

A **compound sentence** consists of two or more independent (main) clauses each containing a subject and a predicate joined by a comma with a coordinating conjunction (**for, and, nor, but, or, yet, so**), a semicolon or semicolon followed by a conjunctive adverb and a comma to express two closely related ideas. Two or more simple sentences connected by a coordinating conjunction exemplify a compound sentence. Do not join a compound sentence with only a comma; this creates a run-on sentence (comma splice). To correct this problem, make two sentences, join two clauses with a semicolon, join two clauses with a semicolon and conjunctive adverb, or join two clauses with a comma and coordinating conjunction.

A **complex sentence** consists of one independent clause (main clause) and at least one dependent (subordinate) clause. Use subordinating conjunctions (**until, while** and **even though**) to link the main clause and subordinate (dependent) clause. A dependent clause must have an independent clause to complete the sentence.

A **compound-complex sentence** consists of at least two independent clauses and one dependent clause joined by semicolons or coordinating conjunctions.

To combine two closely related sentences of equal importance, use a semicolon or coordinating conjunction.

To offer more variety than writing simple sentences, convert a compound sentence into an independent clause and dependent clause to establish an exact relationship.

A **declarative sentence** states an idea of fact or opinion that ends with a period.

An **exclamatory sentence** expresses strong emotions or feelings and ends with an exclamation mark (!).

An **interrogative sentence** asks a question that ends with a question mark (?).

An **imperative sentence** expresses a command or gives an order or directions and ends with a period or exclamation mark (. or !).

Sentence errors to look for when you write include:

Groups of words such as phrases or clauses that do not express a complete thought because of a missing subject or predicate or both; this is known as a sentence fragment.

Correct the sentence fragment by adding a subordinating conjunction, connect the fragment to another sentence as a subordinating clause or add the missing part of the sentence such as subject or verb or both.

Use sentence fragments with quotation marks to create realistic dialogue.

Use correct verb form by matching the subject with the appropriate singular or plural predicate.

A lack of punctuation between two independent clauses creates a run-on, or fused, sentence.

A dependent clause does not represent a complete sentence.

Use a coordinating conjunction, semicolon or a period for two independent clauses.

Use a subordinating conjunction, a semicolon or coordinating conjunction to create a complex sentence.

To emphasize the main idea and build interest in a sentence, put subordinate ideas in modifiers (phrases) or subordinate clauses first, and then present the key thought in the independent clause.

Another way to emphasize the main idea is to put the major point at the beginning of the sentence in the main or independent clause and add subordinate phrases and clauses that develop the major point.

Modifiers, such as adjective, noun or prepositional phrases, do not alter the basic structure of a sentence.

Use uncomplicated sentences (simple) to state complex ideas. Use complex sentence construction to state a series of simple ideas.

Various sentence patterns you can follow:

> Subject and verb (compound)
> Subject, verb and direct object (all may be compound)
> Subject, verb, direct object and objective complement (Advertising made the sales drive a success.)
> Subject, verb, indirect object and direct object
> Subject, verb and subjective complement (predicate nominative, predicate adjective)
> Subject, linking verb and subjective complement (The advertising was effective.)

Invert sentence order of the subject and verb to create questions, exclamations or achieve emphasis. (Have you a pen?)

Sentences introduced by expletives (there, it) put the subject after the verb. It (expletive) is (verb) difficult (complement) to work (subject) in a noisy office. There (expletive) are (verb) certain principles (subject) of drafting.

Simile

A simile expresses a comparison using **like** or **as**.

Slash (/)

A slash separates lines of poetry when written in paragraph form.

Leave a space before and after the slash to show when the line of poetry ends.

Separate dates with slashes (07/04/2004).

Use a slash to show choice or options such as Fahrenheit/ Centigrade, and/or, or teachers/scholars.

Use a slash in fractions or formulas (separate the numerator from the denominator).

Use a slash to separate parts of addresses:

> Ms. Rose Howard/62W
> Pacific Court/Dalton/Ontario/Canada

Use a slash to indicate omitted words or letters (miles per hour, miles/hour; in care of, c/o; without, w/o).

Spelling

Learn spelling rules; know the exceptions. Some words require memorization.

Use memory tricks, mnemonics, to help you remember. Use an acronym—a word created from the first letter in a series of words.

Write down the words over and over. Learn to pronounce each word as you spell it. Use the dictionary to check spelling, pronunciation and definitions of words.

When you add a prefix to a root word, don't add or omit a letter (dissatisfied, illegible, malnutrition, misinformation, misspelled, subtraction, unnatural, unprepared).

Usually in two vowels combinations (**ai, ui, ea**), pronounce the first letter long (a sounds like ay, e sounds like ee, i sounds like eye) and the second letter silent (abstain, acquaint, chaise, cheap, conceal, gear, heal, juice, lead, nuisance, paisley, prevail, refrain, reveal, ruin, steal, suit, traipse).

Some exceptions to the above rule are: porcelain, beauty, healthy, hearse, hearty.

When the word sounds like uh, use **ai,** but if the vowel pair separates the sounds, use **ia** except when words combine **c** or **t** with **ia**, then use the schwa sound (alleviate, beneficial, brilliant, Britain, captain, certain, chieftain, civilian, curtain, familiar, fountain, glacial, guardian, martial, median, menial, villain).

Keep all the letters when you add a suffix unless the word ends in a **y** or a silent **e**.

If the letter before the final **y** is a vowel, don't change the **y** before attaching a suffix (annoyance, enjoyable, boyish, played, relaying). There are some exceptions to the rule that change **y** to **i** (say to said, day to daily, pay to paid, lay to laid, slay to slain).

If the suffix begins with a consonant, retain the silent **e** (atonement) except after the letters **u** or **w** (advertisement, appropriateness, argument, awful, careless, chastely, duly, excitement, graceful, hateful, immediately, lively, lovely, paleness, sincerely, truly).

Some exceptions to the above rule are whole to wholly, judge to judgment, acknowledge to acknowledgment.

If a word ends in **ie**, drop the **e** and change the **i** to **y** (lie to lying, die to dying).

Add **ly** to change an adjective into an adverb.

If the adjective ends in **ic**, add **al** before **ly** (drastically).

If the adjective ends in **ble**, change **ble** to **bly** (able to ably and noble to nobly).

In a one-syllable word, double the final consonant before a suffix beginning with a vowel: **ed, ing, ance, ence, ant, est** (big to biggest).

Double the final consonant for an accented last syllable word with only one consonant (acquit to acquitting, refer to referring, commit to committed).

In words of two or more syllables, double the final consonant only if it is accented.

In a two or more syllable word, double the syllable's final consonant before a suffix beginning with a vowel (deferred or resubmitting).

If a word ends in a consonant, except for **h** or **x,** and has a vowel before it, then double the final consonant before adding **ing**, **er**, **ed, able** or **est** (hop to hopped, hopping, hopper or plan, planner or planning).

If more than one syllable, follow the same rules as for one syllable. Double the final consonant and add the suffix: **ing**, **er, est,** or **ed** (deferred, regretted, regretting and regrettable).

Keep the final **n** when you add **ness** (keenness, leanness).

Keep the final **l** when you add **ly** (formally, regally, legally).

Some exceptions to the doubling rules are: bus to buses, draw to drawing, chagrin to chagrined.

If a word ends in **ic**, insert a **k** after the **c** if the ending begins with **e**, **i** or **y** (mimic to mimicking, picnic to picnicking or panic to panicky, traffic to trafficking).

For words that end in **e**, just add **st** or **r**.

For words that end in **y**, change the **y** to **i** if it follows a consonant, except for the **ing** ending (angry to angrily, beauty to beautiful, hungry to hungriest, funny to funnier, lonely to loneliness, salary to salaries, study to studying).

Do not double the final consonant if it comes after two vowels or another consonant (failed, stooped, warmer, lasting, concealed, abducting, commendable).

Adjectives usually end in **able** if you can trace it back to a noun ending in **ation**, but an exception is **sensible**.

For contractions, insert an apostrophe for the omitted letter or letters (it is—it's, you are—you're, they are—they're, cannot—can't, will not—won't).

Three words end with **ceed: succeed, proceed, and exceed**.

All other words end in **cede** (concede, precede, intercede and accede).

Only one verb ends with **sede: supersede**.

Most words end with **ful** except the word full.

Put i before **e** except after **c. Use ei** if it sounds like **ee**, long **i**, short **e** or **ay** in a word (ceiling, conceit, conceive, counterfeit, deceit, deceive, deign, eight, either, feign, foreign, forfeit, freight, heifer, heinous, height, leisure, neighbor, neither, perceive, receipt, receive, reign, seize, seizure, sheik, sleigh, sleight, stein, seismology, their, veil, vein, weigh, weight, weird).

Spell words with **i** before **e** that make the long **e** sound, short **e** sound, long **i** sound or words that pronounce **c** as **sh** (achieve, ancient, belief, believe, cashier, chief, conscience, deficient, efficient, fiend, fierce, fiery, friend, grief, mischief, niece, notoriety, piece, piety, quiet, relief, retrieve, reprieve, science, series, shriek, sieve, siege, society, sufficient, wield).

Certain words have silent letters:

- ➤ Silent b: debt, doubtable, subtle, climb, lamb, numb, crumb, tomb, dumb, plumb, thumb
- ➤ Silent c: acquire, ascertain, indict
- ➤ Silent g: align, design, gnarled, gnat, gnu, gnash, gnaw, gnome
- ➤ Silent gh: blight, through, throughout
- ➤ Silent h: exhaust, exhibit, ghost, ghastly, ghoul, gherkin, rhetorical
- ➤ Silent t: bankruptcy, listen, mortgage, bristle, gristle, thistle, apostle, wrestle, bustle
- ➤ Silent k: knack, knave, knead, kneel, knapsack, knee, knob, knot, knell, knew, knife, knight, knit, knock, know, knowledge
- ➤ Silent n: autumn
- ➤ Silent p: cupboard, pneumatic, psalm, pseudonym, psychology, psychiatry, ptarmigan, ptomaine
- ➤ Silent s: aisle, isle, island
- ➤ Silent w: whole, answer, wrap, wreath, wrench, wrestle, wrist, write, writhe, wrought, playwright

Some words sound like they have an **i** but instead have a **y** (abyss or paralysis).

Do not divide one-syllable words; generally, do not divide words with six or fewer letters. Divide at the suffix, prefix or hyphen unless essential to the meaning of the word. Do not divide abbreviations and contractions, proper names, company titles, last word of a paragraph or last word on a page of a typewritten manuscript.

With words that end in **e,** when adding **ing, able, ous, ish, ity** or any other suffix beginning with a vowel, usually you will drop the **e** (argue to arguable or arguing, blue to bluish, come to coming, love to loving or lovable, write to writing, please to pleasing or pleasant, hope to hoping, give to giving, virtue to virtuous, opportune to opportunity).

Keep the final e to protect the communication of the word (shoeing, guaranteeing).

Words that end in **ce** or **ge** do not drop the **e** before **able** or **ous** (peace to peaceable) to keep the **c** and **g** sounds soft, like **s** and **j,** as they sound in the original word (courage to courageous, outrage to outrageous, advantage to advantageous, notice to noticeable, charge to chargeable, enforce to enforceable, service to serviceable, trace to traceable, change to changeable, manage to manageable). The letters **c** and **g** are pronounced soft when followed by **e, i,** or **y** (centimeter, centrifuge, central, circle, circulate, circus, cycle, cyclical, cymbal, general, generous, genteel, genius, germ, George, giant, giraffe, gym, gyrate). With other letters, **c** becomes hard sounding the way that **k** and **g** become hard sounding as in gamble, go, gun).

Some words retain the final **e** in order to prevent mispronunciation and confusion of the meaning (hoe to hoeing, shoe to shoeing, toe to toeing, singe to singeing, dye to dyeing, hinge to hingeing).

To make the superlative with words ending in **e**, add **st** or **er** for second best. For words ending in **y**, change the **y** to **i** and add **st** or **er**.

Spell out cardinal numbers expressed as exact quantities (one pencil, two birds).

Spell out single-word ordinal numbers (tenth, first, third).

Spell out numbers from one to ten. Write in figures numbers above ten.

Express units of measurement as figures (5 miles, 35 cubic feet).

Spell out numbers that begin a sentence.

Write out one number as a figure and the other as a word if in the same phrase (five 10-inch rods).

Spell out approximate numbers.

Normally, write percentages as figures.

Write page numbers as figures.

Chapter or volume numbers appear either as figures or written out.

Form plurals of written numbers by adding **s** or **es**. For numbers ending in **y,** drop the **y** and add **ies** (sevens, sixes, twenties).

For plural of figures, add **'s** (6's, 11's).

Do not follow a word representing a number with a figure in parentheses representing the same number.

Year and day of the month written as figures (June 23, 1975, 23 June 1975).

Express hours and minutes as figures when followed by a.m. and p.m. (8:30 a.m., 6:30 p.m.). Spell out hours and minutes not followed by a.m. or p.m. (four o'clock, ten o'clock).

Mixed fractions are expressed as figures (12 ½ inches, 3 ½ miles). Individual fractions are spelled out (one-fourth, five-eighths). For numbers with decimals, write as figures (3.3 meters, 10.5 yards). Spell out street numbers from one to ten (East First Street, Fifth Avenue). Write building numbers as figures except building number one. Write highway numbers as figures (Highway 80).

Homonyms sound the same but have a different meaning and spelling (affect/effect, altar/alter, bare/bear, bloc/block, cite/site/ sight, cord/chord, coarse/course, do/dew, descent/dissent, dual/ duel, heal/heel, led/lead, loan/lone, minor/miner, passed/past, peal/peel, piece/peace, sheer/shear, stationery/stationary, weak/ week, which/witch, right/write). See the usage section for further definitions.

Write compound words as one word or hyphenated (bedroom, courthouse, editor-in-chief, father-in-law, mother-in-law, nevertheless, overcoat).

STYLE

Style represents your distinctive way of writing.

Your audience often helps you determine an appropriate style to produce simple, direct and concise writing.

When you write, focus on the audience's needs, interests and goals.

Understand the values, beliefs and attitudes of the audience.

Communicate a focused idea on a particular topic which will interest your audience and create a favorable impression on the reader.

Present your ideas at a pace that sustains the reader's interest.

Emphasize information the reader should focus on to grasp your point of view or purpose for the prose.

Empathy may help the writer understand someone else's point of view.

Always tell the truth.

The writer should develop his own personae, a unique attitude toward the subject.

Decide on a tone suitable for your audience.

Use unbiased language in your writing.

Positive rather than negative statements create conciseness.

Use appropriate words to emphasize your intended mood.

Make every word add meaning to your idea; eliminate unneeded words.

Your writing starts with a specific denotation and connotation for each word in each sentence.

Denotation represents the explicit meaning of a word from the dictionary.

Connotation, emotional overtones of positive, negative or neutral words, conveys the exact meaning you want to express to your audience.

A **euphemism** substitutes an offensive word for a more subtle, less harsh or distasteful word.

A **dysphemism** substitutes a positive or neutral expression or word with a negative or unpleasant word or expression.

An **antonym** represents a word opposite from and a **synonym** represents a word similar to your original word.

Use words the audience knows and understands to convey your exact meaning.

Find the simplest word to express your exact meaning.

Define key terms or expressions the reader may not understand.

Define terms by classifying the features of words into categories. Use a familiar word or phrase to define your word. Avoid using definitions that include terms unfamiliar to the reader.

Use synonyms and euphemisms carefully to avoid unwanted connotations and overused nouns or pronouns.

Each word will affect your clarity and impact on your audience.

Reduce occupational jargon and buzz words unless you feel the audience already understands the specific words.

Replace vague or abstract words, phrases or clichés with specific, precise, concrete words that provide richness, complexity and uniqueness to convey your intended meaning.

Specific, illustrative words communicate your thoughts clearly.

Descriptive, detailed words create interest, suspense, form vivid mental pictures and help the reader understand your message or key points.

Would you rather read about food, birds and colors, or chicken cutlets, bald eagles and sapphire blue?

The more your words stimulate the reader's senses (feel, taste, sound and touch), the greater the impact of your writing.

Abstract or vague words generally do not stimulate the senses, but specific, precise, concrete words do.

Choice of words determines tone, voice, diction, sentence length and overall structure.

Repetition of key words or ideas helps to achieve emphasis of your ideas.

Reduce confusion or ambiguity by positioning words or groups of words to show your intended relationship in the sentence.

Write clear, complete and correct sentences that suit your topic, purpose and audience.

Relate ideas in a logical order to create unity, balance, coherence and cohesion.

Style topics to consider:

> Emphasis and importance
> Position of a sentence, paragraph, report
> Repetition of key words and phrases
> Sentence type: simple, compound, complex
> Climatic order of ideas or facts within a sentence
> Punctuation, dash, intensifiers, setting an item apart
> Italics, capital letters, underlining
> Direct statement (most important, foremost)
> First and last words stand out in a sentence or paragraph in a report
> An independent clause in a complex sentence creates emphasis in the sentence
> Different lengths create emphasis

Prominent words usually start at the end or beginning of the sentence.

Decide what sentence structure best expresses your thoughts.

Use simple and complex sentences to vary the length and type of sentences to create variety and interest in the most concise and simplest form.

Simple sentences create emphasis after a series of complex sentences.

Simple sentences increase the reader's understanding of complicated subjects or topics.

Poor sentence structure breaks down clarity and communication.

Short, direct sentences that are to the point may suggest importance and equal emphasis with no subordination. Too many short sentences together create choppy, staccato thoughts or a boring, repetitive rhythm.

Too many sentences connected by coordinating conjunctions create monotony too.

Expand sentences with phrases and clauses.

Watch for stereotypical phrases.

Audiences tend to remember beginning or ending clauses.

Link related ideas with independent and subordinate clauses.

Emphasize the most important idea of the sentence in the main clause and less important or supporting ideas in the subordinate clause.

Use complex sentences to link ideas or combine sentences with similar ideas.

Generally, do not separate the subject and verb by a phrase or a clause.

Add adjectives and adverbs to emphasize key words.

Break your writing pattern with commands, questions or dialogue.

People do not necessarily speak (dialogue) in complete sentences.

Use dialogue with fragments; it's more natural than using full sentences.

Direct quotes from a source text add legitimacy to your writing.

Use the active voice unless the passive voice creates a specific meaning.

In the active voice, the subject performs the action named by the verb.

In the passive voice, the subject receives the action in a subordinating position.

Revise passive voice sentences that begin with expletives such as **it is, there is, there are** or **there were** with an action verb.

Use repetition of sound, words, phrases or grammatical structure to create rhythm, clarity and emphasis of key points or to link related ideas.

For example, "We cannot dedicate, we cannot consecrate, we cannot hallow this ground ..." demonstrates repetition and parallel structure in President Lincoln's writing.

Use parallel construction to help the reader recognize similar content or function.

Effective writing requires relevant support to prove your point.

Use statistics, facts, key details, definitions, examples or quotations to reinforce your point of view or message.

Prove your facts and statistics through observation, experimentation or reference sources.

When you want to show strong emotion, use vivid adjectives and verbs instead of interjections and exclamation points.

Rearrange sentences to remove singular pronouns.

Use fewer commas to create concise sentences.

When choosing words, phrases or combining thoughts in a sentence, decide whether a comma, semicolon, colon, connecting word(s) or period would create your intended meaning.

Summarize your conclusions with strong evidence, facts and other key information to strengthen your point of view.

Study famous writers' patterns and then apply them yourself.

Readers appreciate an opportunity to laugh or smile. Humorous quotations or anecdotes add to almost any topic.

Use a dash before the last word of a sentence to add force to your meaning.

Form words and sentences into patterns so your emphasized ideas come to a natural high point. Form a pattern by repeating a word, phrase, clause or sentence. Follow three or four long sentences with a short one. Put a few short sentences before a long one. Write words in a rhythmical pattern or endless combinations of sentence variety. Punctuation, figures of speech, tone, attitude toward subject and audience, all contribute to your style of writing.

Tone

Tone, one's attitude toward the subject and audience, suggests how the author states ideas, a point of view, message, style and language. The writer conveys hope, happiness, insecurity, disrespect, sarcasm, irony, playfulness, sincerity or insincerity, authority, humor, gloom, threats and positive or negative thoughts toward the subject and the reader.

Transition

Coherent writing consists of ideas related to each other in a logical manner. Transitions can be a paragraph, a sentence, an expression, a phrase or a word that shows a logical relationship between paragraphs and sentences. Different transitional expressions signal to the reader how one idea links to the others. Appropriate transitions convey ideas smoothly and clearly.

Types of transitions:

To add information as a transition use: **also, and, besides, finally, further, furthermore, in addition to, moreover, next, then.**

For examples use: **for example, for instance, namely, specifically.**

Chronological order use: **first, firstly, second, secondly, third, thirdly, forth, next, subsequently, immediately, later, eventually, in the future, currently, now, during, meanwhile, before, soon, afterwards, at length, finally, then, suddenly, after, while, at last, in the meantime.**

For contrast use: **nevertheless, nonetheless, yet, in contrast, on the contrary, still, however, on the other hand.**

For comparison use: **in comparison, similarly, likewise, in the same way.**

For concession use: **naturally, granted, certainly, to be sure, of course.**

For place use: **in the distance, here, there, at the side of, next to, adjacent, in the front, in the back.**

For result use: **due to this, so, accordingly, consequently, as a result, therefore.**

For summary use: **finally, in conclusion, in summary, in brief, as a result, hence, on the whole, in short.**

USAGE

Apt means natural tendency.

About means approximately.

Around means starting at one point, coming back to the same point.

Accept, a verb, means to receive, consent to, admit willingly or take something offered.

Except, normally a preposition, means to take out, exclude or leave out.

Adapt means adjust to new conditions.
Adopt means take as your own that was not originally yours.
Adept means highly skilled.

Admittance means allow to enter.
Admission means fee paid to enter; owning up to an accusation or statement; the act of being allowed to enter a group, society, college or school.

Advice means counsel or recommendation.
Advise means to provide advice.

Affect represents a verb that means to impress, influence, to move on to, act on, assume the character or appearance, to put on.

Effect represents a noun that means result or consequence, outcome, fulfillment, accomplishment, make an impression.

Effect represents a verb that means to bring about; to execute; often in the face of difficulties or obstacles, to cause. Use **made** as a verb instead of effect.

Affinity means attraction of two people; does not mean ability or aptitude.

Agree to means give consent.
Agree with means in accord.

Aggravate means to make something worse.
Annoy means to irritate, exasperate but not aggravate.

Avoid using **above to** when referring to an illustration, previous passage or table; may cause distraction or confusion.

Altogether means completely, entirely, all.
All together means all of us, of them together, acting together, all in the same place.

All-round or **all-around** means comprehensive or versatile.
All around means to circle.

Do not use **most** for **almost**.

Allusion means implied or indirect reference to something not specifically mentioned.
Delusion means special sense to describe the false and fantastic ideas of insane people.
Illusion means deceptive appearance like an optical illusion, mistaken perception, false image.
Refer means a direct reference to something.

Already, an adverb, expresses passed time.
All ready means prepared.

Also, an adverb, represents in addition. Do not use **also** as a connective for **and** or other sentence connectives.

Use **amount** with noncountable things (bulk).

Use **number** with countable things.

Do not use **A and/or B**, change to A or B or both.
Do not use **as well as** and **both** in the same sentence.

Attribute, used as a verb, means point to a cause or source.
Attribute, used as a noun, means quality or characteristic.

Augment means increased or to magnify in size, degree of effect.
Supplement means to add something to replace a deficiency.

Awhile, an adverb, means for a short time.
A while, a noun phrase, means a period of time.

Bad, an adjective, follows linking verbs.
Badly, an adverb, means in a disadvantageous way.

Balance means state of equilibrium, amount in bank account.
Remainder means what is left over.

Do not use **being that** or **being as** for **since** or **because.**

Beside means next to or at the side of.
Besides means except or in addition to.

Borrow means accept something as a loan from a person.

Between, a preposition, means with two people or two items. Use the objective form of the personal pronoun **me** (pronouns are objects of the preposition such as between you and me).

Among means with three or more people or things or have a large number of things; people and the writer or speaker distinguish between any two of them.

Bet means wager.
Beat means to win, conquer, defeat.

Bring means to carry, come with something toward the speaker or listener.
Take means to carry away something from the speaker.

Bunch represents things that grow or are formed together, not people.
Use **group** for people.

Can means capability.
May means possibility or permission.

Capital means city, seat of government, punishable by death.
Capitol means the building where a state legislature meets, the state house. Use small **c** for state building and large **C** when used for the Capitol Building in Washington, D.C.

Cite means acknowledge or quote an authority.
Site means place or plot of land where something is located.
Sight means ability to see.

Childish means unattractive features of children (silliness, stubbornness, temper tantrum).
Childlike means best, most attractive characteristics of children (sweetness, innocence, faith).

Complement means portion, which fills up or completion.
Compliment used as a verb or a noun, to praise, commendation, congratulation.

Compose means create, make up the whole.
Comprise means include.

Conscience means ability to decide what is morally right and wrong.
Conscious means aware of, awake.

Consul means official who represents a government in a foreign country.
Counsel means give advice, an advisor.
Council means a body of people serving in a legal, administrative or advisory capacity.

Contemptible means deserving of contempt, despicable.
Contemptuous means regarding others as contemptible, looking down on them with distain and scorn.

Continual means repeated often.
Continuous means without a stop.

Criterion means an established standard for judging or testing.
Criteria represents the plural form of criterion.

Definite or **definitive** both apply to what is precisely defined. **Definitive** more often refers to what is complete and authoritative.

Diagnosis means analysis of something or conclusions reached by analysis.
Prognosis means a prediction or forecast.

Differ from suggests that two things are not alike.
Differ with suggests disagreement between two people.

Discover means find something already there before you came upon it.
Invent means create something new.

Disinterested means no desire to gain something for oneself.
Uninterested means not interested.

Despite suggests an effort to avoid blame.

Dual means belonging to or shared by two.
Duel means a contest between two people fought with deadly weapons.

Eminent means outstanding or distinguished.
Imminent means about to happen.
Immanent means inherent or Deity sustains all material in existence.

Explicit means expressed directly with precision and clarity.
Implicit means found within a statement, not directly expressed.

Do not use **fact** to refer to matters of judgment or opinion.

Famous means well known.
Notorious means well known but in an unfavorable light.

Farther means measurable distance.
Further indicates degree or extent.

Fewer refers to number.
Less refers to amount or degree.

For refers to a period of time. (I have worked for ten years.)
Since refers to the start of a period. (I have been working since 7 o'clock.)

117

Formally means in accordance with certain rules or forms.
Formerly means in the past or at another time.
Former refers to the first of the two mentioned.

Fortuitous happens by chance or accident.
Fortunate happens by good fortune.

Foreword, a noun, makes an introductory statement at the beginning of a book or other work.
Forward, an adjective or adverb, represents toward the front.
Preface represents a statement by the author about the purpose, background or scope of the book or report.

Good is an adjective. (Mary has a good voice, she sings well.)
Well, an adjective, describes health.
Well, an adverb, describes how. (How does Mary sing? She sings well.)

Use **himself** and **themselves**, not **theirselves**.

Human means characteristic of man.
Humane means tender, kind, compassionate.

Illegible means cannot read.
Ineligible means does not meet the required qualifications.

Immigrate means to come into another country after leaving one's native land.
Emigrate means to leave your native land.

In common means when two or more people or things share it or possess it jointly.

Mutual means shared, but it usually implies something given and received reciprocally, used with reference to only two people or parties.

Imply means to hint.
Infer means to find out by reasoning, to draw a conclusion from facts or evidence.

Ingenious means clever, skillful, resourceful or inventive.
Ingenuous means frank, sincere, honest or open.

Use **regarding**, not **in regards to**.

118

Intelligent means alert, wise.
Intelligible means capable of being understood.

Lend means give something to a person with the expectation of its return.
Latest means most recent.
Last means the final one.

Lay, a transitive verb, means to put something down, which always takes an object. Ask the question **what;** if an answer, use **lay.** If no answer, use **lie.**
Lie, an intransitive verb, means to recline (lie, lay, have lain) and does not need an object.
Lie means to tell an untruth (lie, lied, have lied).

Avoid the use of **like** for **as** or **as if.**

Learn means to receive knowledge.
Teach means to impart or give knowledge.

Leave as a verb means depart, allow to remain, go away or abandon; as a noun is used as granted a leave of absence.
Let means to permit or to allow.

Like, a preposition, means similar; use with a noun or pronoun that is not followed by a verb. (The new supervisor behaves like a novice.)

As, a conjunction, is used before clauses; at the time that, what, because. (He acted as though he owned the company.)

Likely means idea of probability, it may happen.
Liable means possibility of an unpleasant happening.

Number means you can count the things you write about.
Amount means quantities that cannot be counted; consider the size of things.

Off means removing something on a person; don't use **off of.**

Persons refers to individual people, thought of separately.
People identifies a large or anonymous group.

Persecute means to annoy, to plague, to hunt down, to bring unhappiness and suffering.

Prosecute means to carry out a legal action.

Principal means the main, primary or most important, money which earns interest paid or the head of a school or court proceeding, or the main person in a company.
Principle means belief, truth, policy, conviction or rule.

Pour means to fill into something.
Spill means something comes out of, such as water from a cup.

Practical means useful and valuable, tried and tested.
Practicable means workable.

Precede means to go before.
Proceed means to go forward.

Instead of **re** (in reference to), use **subject**.

Refer means a direct reference to something.

Use **regardless**, not **irregardless.**

Raise, a transitive verb, means to move something higher, act as a parent toward children, make larger or greater.
Rise, an intransitive verb, means to stand up, ascend, increase in level.

Respectfully means showing respect or honor to someone.
Respectively refers to a number of items taken in order.

Rout means to defeat completely.
Route means a road.

Stand means upright, to become upright, bear something.
Stay means do not move or go away, remain.

Stationary means remaining in one place.
Stationery means writing paper or envelopes.

Statue means an image of a person.
Statute means a law.

Use **this kind** or **that kind**, **these** or **those kinds.**

Verbs

A verb describes the visible or mental action or state of being of the subject.

A **transitive** verb asks **who** or **what** after the verb and requires a direct object. For example, the basketball player threw the ball. **Ball** is the object of **threw**, the transitive verb.

An **intransitive** verb does not require a direct object to complete the sentence. For example, the teacher spoke.

Principal Verb Forms

The basic forms of a verb consist of the infinitive, present participle, past and past participle. The infinitive form represents the **to** form of the verb. The present participle represents the helping verb form **is**. The past verb form represents the regular verb form with **ed** or **d** or the irregular verb form. The past participle represents **has**, **has** or **have** with the past regular or irregular verb form.

For example: The verb, **watch**, becomes:

Infinitive: watch
Present participle: is watching
Past: watched
Past participle: have watched or has watched

Irregular present tense verbs do not form the past tense and past participle by adding **d** or **ed**. The verb may change spelling (change a vowel and add **n** or **en** [**begin, began, begun**], change vowel, add **d** or **t** [lose, lost, lost] or some verbs do not change [set or put]). Go to the end of the verb section for examples of irregular verb changes.

A helping verb, or auxiliary verb, added before a main verb helps indicate mood, tense and voice to form a passive voice or verb phrase; it requires the subjective case with any form of **is, are, am, do, does, did, have, has, had, shall, will, would, can, could, may, might** or **must.** You may separate the helping verb from the main verb.

A **linking verb** joins the subject and predicate but does not show action and may express a state or a condition or it may define the subject further. These verbs link a noun, pronoun or adjective to the subject. The word linked to the subject is called a **subject complement**, which always refers to the subject of the linking verb. The teacher is a **female**. The subject complement, female, refers to the subject, teacher. **Is** represents the linking verb. A word that describes the subject after the linking verb is called an **adjective complement.** For example, the teacher is happy. **Happy**, the adjective complement, refers to the teacher. Common linking verbs use the verb forms of **be** (**am, is, are, was, were, be, being** or **been** and verb phrases ending in **be, being** or **been**), feel, grow, seem, smell, remain, appear, sound, stay, look or taste. Linking verbs are inherently intransitive since they connect a subject to a modifier or a complement.

Case

A verb in the subjective case describes the subject.

The verb case describes **who** or **what** experiences the action: the first person, person speaking, **me**; second person, person spoken to, **you**; and third person, person being spoken about, **he** or **she**.

Tense

Verb tense describes when something occurs, either present, past or future.

Make sure the verb tense matches the singular or plural subject. Do not mix tenses in a sentence. If you write in the past tense, use the present tense for continuous true information. If the subjects differ in number, the verb agrees with the nearest subject. (Neither my brother nor my sisters are going.) A singular subject requires a singular verb. Plural subjects require plural verbs. A compound subject joined by **or** or **nor** takes a singular verb if each subject is singular. **Either, every, neither, everyone, anyone,** and **nobody** use singular verbs. Compound subjects use plural verbs. Depending on the sentence, use singular or plural verbs with **all, more** or **some**.

Present tense expresses action or is a statement about something in the present, something that happens repeatedly (timetables, programs) or that is a permanent situation. (You eat fish. We learn Spanish.) Express a general truth in the present tense.

The **present progressive form** shows continuing, unfinished action, prior arrangement or a temporary situation by inserting an auxiliary verb (I am; he, she, it is; we, you, they are) and add the **ing form** of the verb. (I am going to the movies. You are eating fish now. We are learning Spanish now.)

The **present perfect tense** expresses action or is a statement about something occurring at no definite time in the past, after the simple past that continues into the future or that has a bearing on the present by adding **have (I, we, they, you)** or **has (he, she, it)** to the past participle. (I have eaten fish. She has learned Spanish.)

The **present perfect progressive tense** expresses action that began in the past and continues in the present. Use this tense to ask or say how long an activity still occurs. Use **have** or **has** with **been** plus the **ing** form of the verb. (How long have you been eating fish? I have been eating fish for the past six days. How long has she been studying Spanish? She has been learning Spanish for the past two years.)

The **past tense** expresses action or is a statement about something that occurred in the past but did not continue into the future. (You studied Spanish. We learned Spanish.) For regular verbs, generally, add **d** or **ed** to the verb to form the past tense. For irregular verbs, memorize the verb form. Past tense of **be:** I, he, she, it **was**; we, you, they **were**. Use **when** plus past tense in a question. (When did you eat fish? I ate fish yesterday.)

The **past progressive form** represents the action or situation already started but not finished. Use **was** or **were** and the **ing** form of the verb. (I was eating fish this morning. We were studying Spanish at 9 o'clock.) Often one will use the past tense and past progressive together to express something that happened in the middle of something else. (When I was eating fish this morning, a bear entered my campsite.)

The **past perfect tense** expresses action or is a statement about something completed in the past before some other past action or event by using **had** with the past participle. (After I had eaten fish for a week, I then started to eat meat. She had studied Spanish for the past year and then traveled to Spain.)

The **past perfect progressive tense** expresses action or is a statement about something that began in the past and is formed by using the auxiliary verbs **had been** with the progressive form (**ing**) of the verb. (I had been eating fish. She had been studying Spanish.)

The **simple future tense** expresses action or is a statement about something that will occur sometime in the future by adding **will, would** or **shall** to the present tense verb. (I will eat fish. I will learn Spanish.) Use **will** when offering, agreeing, promising or asking to do something. Use **shall** in questions. (Shall we eat fish tonight? Shall I learn Spanish?) Use **shall** with **I** and **we**. Do not use **will** when somebody has already decided to do something in the future. Use **will** when the speaker decides to do something without prior intent of the new action.

The **future progressive tense** expresses continuing action in the future by adding **will be, would be** or **shall be** to the progressive form of the verb. (I will be eating fish. She will be studying Spanish.)

The **future perfect tense** describes a future action completed at a certain time in the future, before another action or a finished future condition before another action by adding **will have, would have** or **will have been** before the past participle. (I will have eaten fish by the end of the day. She will have studied Spanish by the end of the summer.)

The **future perfect progressive tense** describes a continuing future action finished at some time in the future or before another finished action or event by adding **will have been, would have been** or **shall have been** before the progressive form of the verb. (I will have been eating fish by the end of the day. I will have been studying Spanish by the end of the summer.)

Conjugate a Verb

Match the pronoun (I, you, he, she, it, we, you [plural] and they) to the correct verb form for each tense.

For example: Conjugate the irregular verb **go**.

Present infinitive: to go
Past infinitive: to have gone
Infinitive: go
Present participle: going
Past: went
Past participle: gone

Present Tense

Singular: I go; you go; he, she, it goes
Plural: we go, you go, they go
Present progressive: I am going (auxiliary verb plus going), etc.

Past Tense

Singular: I went; you went; he, she, it went
Plural: we went, you went, they went
Past progressive: I was going, etc.

Future Tense

Singular: I will (shall) go; you will (shall) go; he, she, it will (shall) go
Plural: we will (shall) go, you will (shall) go, they will (shall) go
Future progressive: I will be going, etc.

Present Perfect Tense

Singular: I have gone; you have gone; he, she, it has gone
Plural: we have gone, you have gone, they have gone
Present perfect progressive: I have been going, etc.

Past Perfect Tense

Singular: I had gone; you had gone; he, she, it had gone
Plural: we had gone, you had gone, they had gone
Past perfect progressive: I had been going, etc.

Future Perfect Tense

Singular: I will (shall) have gone; you will have gone; he, she, it will have gone
Plural: we will have gone, you will have gone, they will have gone
Future perfect progressive: I will have been going, etc.

Mood

Indicative, imperative or subjunctive verbs express mood or attitude toward the action or subject.

Indicative mood is used when one makes a statement or asks a question.

Imperative mood expresses commands, direct requests, suggestions or is an entreaty with an implied subject, **you,** or indefinite pronoun. (Go find the book.) Use the simple form of the verb.

The **subjunctive mood** expresses conditions contrary to fact, recommendations, speculations and indirect requests or wishes. Use **be** with singular and plural present subjunctive and **were** for the singular and plural past subjunctive forms. (I suggest that she **be** added to the list. I wish she **were** here.)

Voice

Voice shows whether the subject performed the action or received the action.

Use the **active voice** when the subject performs the action. Name the thing performing the action first.

Verbs that express action performed by the subject are called action verbs. (The teacher **read** the book.)

Turn a passive voice of a verb in a sentence into an active voice by turning a noun into a verb. (Bob is reading a book about world history. Bob reads a world history book.)

Using active voice creates fewer words and direct sentences.

An example of active voice: I eat fish. I study Spanish.

Use passive voice when the action is performed upon the subject or the subject is acted upon.

Use **passive voice** when you do not want to assign blame or emphasize who or what performed the action by moving the object of the sentence ahead of the verb where it becomes the subject and the main verb becomes a past participle expressed by the appropriate form of **be**.

Use passive voice when you do not know who performed the action, or to bury the subject or performer of the action in expletives or prepositional phrases.

Use passive voice to give more importance to the facts or receiver of the action.

The passive voice consists of some form of the verb **to be** and the past participle (**be, being, was, were, been, am, are** and **is**).

An example of passive voice: The fish was eaten by me. I was studying Spanish.

Do not confuse the passive voice with the past tense.

Will the use of the passive voice clarify or obscure your meaning of the sentence?

IRREGULAR VERB FORMS

Memorize the irregular verb forms: the present form, past and past participle of irregular verbs.

Depending on the person speaking, add **have** or **has** to the past participle. (I have gone to the movie. He has gone to the movie.)

Present	Past	Past Participle
burst	burst	burst
bet	bet	bet
rid	rid	rid

hit	hit	hit
do	did	done
see	saw	seen
go	went	gone
lie	lay	lain
lay	laid	laid
arise	arose	arisen
bear	bore	born, borne
beat	beat	beaten
become	became	become
begin	began (begun)	begun
bend	bent	bent
bid	bid	bid
bite	bit	bitten
bleed	bled	bled
blow	blew	blown
break	broke	broken
breed	bred	bred
bring	brought	brought
buy	bought	bought
catch	caught	caught
choose	chose	chosen
ding	dinged	dinged
come	came	come
cost	cost	cost
creep	crept	crept
deal	dealt	dealt
dig	dug	dug
dive	dived, dove	dived
do	did	done
draw	drew	drawn
drink	drank (drunk)	drunk
drive	drove	driven
eat	ate	eaten
fall	fell	fallen
feed	fed	fed
feel	felt	felt
fight	fought	fought
find	found	found
flee	fled	fled
fling	flung	flung

fly	flew	flown
forget	forgot	forgotten
forgive	forgave	forgiven
freeze	froze	frozen
get	got	gotten or got
give	gave	given
go	went	gone
hang	hung	hung
hang (execute)	hanged	hanged
hide	hid	hidden
hold	held	held
hurt	hurt	hurt
kneel	knelt	knelt
know	knew	known
lay	laid	laid
lead	led	led
lie (horizontal)	lay	lain
lie (falsehood)	lied	lied
lose	lost	lost
prove	proved	proved, proven
ride	rode	ridden
ring	rang	rung
run	ran	run
say	said	said
see	saw	seen
seek	sought	sought
sell	sold	sold
send	sent	sent
set	set	set
shake	shook	shaken
shine	shone, shined	shone, shined
shoot	shot	shot
show	showed	shown or showed
shrink	shrank (shrunk)	shrunk
sing	sang (sung)	sung
sink	sank (sunk)	sunk
sit	sat	sat
slay	slew	slain
sleep	slept	slept
slide	slid	slid
sling	slung	slung

slink	slunk	slunk
speak	spoke	spoken
speed	sped	sped
spend	spent	spent
spin	spun	spun
spring	sprang	sprung
stand	stood	stood
steal	stole	stolen
stick	stuck	stuck
sting	stung	stung
stride	strode	stridden
strike	struck	stricken, struck
string	strung	strung
strive	strove	striven
swear	swore	sworn
sweep	swept	swept
swim	swam (swum)	swum
swing	swung	swung
take	took	taken
teach	taught	taught
tear	tore	torn
tell	told	told
think	thought	thought
tread	trod	trod, trodden
throw	threw	thrown
wake	waked, woke	waked, woken
wear	wore	worn
weave	wove	woven
win	won	won
wind	wound	wound
wring	wrung	wrung
write	wrote	written

Vocabulary

The more words you know, the greater the opportunity to express yourself more efficiently to others through speaking or writing.

Build your vocabulary by reading and reviewing the surrounding text (sentences or paragraph) of the unfamiliar word to determine the meaning. You probably can guess the meaning of a word by the context of the surrounding words.

Look up unknown words in the dictionary and review the list periodically.

Find the exact meaning of the word in the sentence.

Write down the word on flashcards to test yourself until the word becomes part of your vocabulary.

Use a thesaurus to learn similar words and relationships.

Once you learn the new word, use it when you speak.

Word parts consist of prefixes, suffixes and root words.

A **root word** represents the direct meaning of the word.

agon – struggle, contest
aud – hear
bell – war
ben – good
bio – life
cap – head
ced – go
chron – time
cis, cid – to cut
contra – against
cred – believe
dem – people
dict – say
duc – lead
fer – bear or carry
fid – faith
flux, flu – to flow

gen – race or kind
cog, gno – to know
greg – crowd
loq – speak
mid, mis – to send
med – middle
nom – name
path – feelings
phobe – fear
ped, pod – foot
ped – child
phil – love
rog – to ask
simul – copy
spic, spec – see
tang, tac, tig – touch
tract – draw, pull
ject – to throw or send
soph – wisdom
ten – hold
trib – to give
urb – city
ver – truth
vid – see
viv – life

A **prefix** is a letter or letters placed in front of a root word that changes or adds to the meaning of the root word.

Separate the prefix ending with a vowel and same vowel root word with a hyphen (co-operate, re-elect, re-enter).

ab – from away
ad – to, forward
ante – before, in front of
anti – against, opposed to (hyphenated when joined to proper noun or words beginning with **i**)
bi – two or every two (biannual, every two years)
circ – around
co – together
con – together, with
contr – against

de – down, away from
dec – ten
dis – undo, do the opposite
eu – good, well
ex – away from, out of
in – usually cause the word following to take opposite meaning.
il – not, opposite
inter – between
mal – bad
meta – beyond
mis – badly, wrong
non – not, without, opposite
over – excessive, extreme, extra, above
pre – before
post – after, later
pro – before, substitute, earlier than
pseudo – false or counterfeit (joined to a root word without a hyphen unless root word begins with a capital letter)
quasi – somewhat or partial, usually hyphenated in combinations
re – again, back
retro – again, back
semi – half of or twice within a period
sub – under
sym, syn – together, with
trans – across
tri – three
un – opposite
under – less than, below, subordinate

A **suffix** added to the end of the root word changes the meaning and identifies its part of speech in the sentence.

Noun endings

escence – state of
ism – state or doctrine of, action, process, characteristic behavior
ist – one who practices a particular skill or profession, belief
ite –mineral, rock, ore, descendant or follower
ity – state of being
ment – quality
tion – act or state of
ry, y – state of

Adjective endings

able – capable
ian – one who is or does
ic – causing, making
ile – pertaining to
ious – having the quality of
ive – having the nature of
less – without

Verb endings

able – capable of (adj)
ate – to make (verb)
ian – one who is or does (adj)
ic – causing (adj)
ify – to make (verb)
ile – pertaining to (adj)
ious – having the quality of (adj)
ism – state or doctrine of (noun)
ist – one who (noun)
ity – state of being (noun)
ive – having the nature of (adj)
ize – to bring about, to subject to an action (verb)

Antonyms represent words opposite in meaning to the compared word.

Synonyms represent words similar in meaning to the compared word.

Denotation of the word represents the dictionary meaning.

Connotation of the word represents the tone or exact meaning of the word.

Homonyms are words that sound the same but have different meanings (see and sea).

Learn the derivatives of words.

Divide:

- ➤ syllables between double consonants

- ➤ syllables after a prefix and before a suffix

- ➤ syllables after a vowel if the vowel has a long sound

- ➤ after the consonant if the vowel sound is short

- ➤ words into syllables

WRITING PROCESS

Step One: Planning

What is your subject, purpose, reason or specific goal for your communication through writing?

Do you clearly understand the subject for your writing project?

Do you plan to explain, describe, persuade, narrate, analyze a particular topic or entertain your reader?

Create instant interest for the reader or they may not read the remainder of your writing.

Once you have decided on a subject, have you determined your topic, thesis or theme, which is your specific issue or central point you will share with your audience?

Define the reader by age, education, gender, geography, heritage, interests, knowledge on the subject and sexual orientation, socio-economic status or other key characteristics of the audience.

Let your audience and subject help you determine your tone. What type of diction, formal or informal, and what position will you use on the specific topic?

Try brainstorming or free writing to generate ideas. Do you have any related experiences or observations? Use your rich storehouse of experience to spark the reader's imagination.

Write down all ideas (words, phrases) on paper and do not worry about grammar or the logic of your thoughts. Keep the ideas related to your topic. Put your ideas into an order which focuses on your topic or point of view.

Are there any time or length constraints of the writing project?

Once you have your ideas on paper, draw lines to connect ideas or show relationships.

These ideas may stimulate you to go in a different direction.

Generate an intelligence diagram.

Charting your ideas may help to relate your ideas.

Ask the questions who, what, where, why and how about your topic.

Narrow your subject by reviewing several viewpoints from your generated related ideas and details.

Do you have a title?

A specific writing strategy is to arrange your entire writing in a question-and-answer format.

Step Two: Research

Find reliable resources for data, facts, statistics, expert opinions, anecdotes or other details for your intended writing project.

Reliable evidence creates powerful, convincing writing.

Step Three: Outline

During this step, put similar ideas together from your research.

Eliminate unrelated ideas and place specific ideas under each general idea.

Determine the best way to organize your material.

Emphasize your key points by placing them in positions of greatest importance (use a new paragraph for each key point).

Your specific details should justify your general statements to create persuasive writing.

Use detailed facts, examples and assertions backed by evidence.

Find the key facts: who, what, where, when, how and why.

Facts represent something true or that happened for certain.

Prove facts through direct observation, experimentation or a reference source.

Decide what information to present first, second, third, etc. in a logical order.

Logical writing creates effective writing.

Show a clear pattern of organization and unity among your sentences, paragraphs and essay.

Transition provides continuity and clarity between sentences or between paragraphs.

Arrange the information in a chronological order, order of importance, order of impression, compare and contrast, cause and effect, spatial order or another methodology.

Differentiate between facts and opinions.

Your opinions should relate to your organized display of facts, details and evidence.

Outline Form

    I. First main idea (main idea indicated by Roman numeral)
        A. Detail (division within a main idea indicated by capital letters)
            1. Reason or example (subdivision within a division indicated by Arabic numerals)
                a. Detail (specific information for each subdivision by lower case letters)
                b. Detail
                    i. detail (identify information for each lowercase letter with a small Roman numeral)
                    ii. detail
            2. Reason or example
                a. Detail
                b. Detail

B. Detail
    1. Reason or example
      a. Detail
      b. Detail
II. Second Main Idea

Step Four: Draft

Once you have your outline, generate your topic sentences from each main idea. Write the remaining sentences from your detailed breakdown for each main paragraph idea with logical and easy-to-read supporting sentences for the topic sentence. Write the introduction last and start on any part of the outline.

Step Five: Revise and Edit

Once you have drafted your writing, go to the writing checklist for revision. Rethink your ideas. Add, cut, move and rewrite to improve unity, logical order and coherence of your message to the reader. Edit for spelling, grammar, punctuation, capitalization and usage.

Does your writing stay within the established scope of your topic?

Step Six: Proofread

After your revision and edit, have your writing proofread by someone other than you.

The proofreader looks for spelling, grammatical and usage errors. Read each letter slowly. Read each sentence, starting from the end of your written material. Reading backwards allows the proofreader to concentrate on the mechanical errors without content distractions. Read the writing aloud while another person follows with a written copy. Say the punctuation marks and spell out all names. Reread the material for content separately.

Does the writing follow a logical sequence?

Other Works by George Kingston:

Goldilocks Makes Friends
(ISBN: 0-9669852-0-6)

Have you or your children ever wondered what happened to Goldilocks after she ran away from the three bears' house? The delightful answer to this mystery is in the telling of **Goldilocks Makes Friends,** a book complete with an activity section of fun puzzles to solve and pictures to color of the characters you and your children just came to know through this timeless story.

The Exciting Adventures of Hydra and Muste Otter
(ISBN: 0-9669852-1-4)

Diana Guerrero, book reviewer for arkanimals.com, wrote the following review of the book.

> If you want your child to have fun learning about sea animals, then this is a must read. The book has beautiful photographs and fun drawings. The name of each character has roots in animal classification (which I thought was a very clever learning tool) and the story conveys important facts about the animal life contained within. The story was fun and educational. These animal adventures are sure to be off on another adventure soon based on the ending. The only weakness I found was that the book was a bit anthropomorphic for me, but kids will love it. As an animal professional, the specific part I had trouble with were the humans (biologists) feeding the otters in the wild (not a good idea) and the part where the otters ride the orca on his back (transient orcas eat mammals). The big plus of this book, beyond the breathtaking photos, is that the author included clever learning aids in the activity section. If you are an educator or home schooler, you will love it! Inside

is a hidden word challenge, a word scramble, a crossword puzzle, questions, a memory game, a sleuth activity, a glossary and classification section and more. Don't worry, an answer key is included.

James A. Cox, from the Midwest Book Review, writes:

> The book is a wondrous, full-color, activities-enhanced storybook for young readers about two otter friends and their day-to-day life. Filled with gorgeous photography and educational information about sea creatures, the food chain and how mammals can survive in the cold and sometimes harsh waters, *The Exciting Adventures of Hydra and Muste Otter* is as informationally enriching as it is fascinatingly entertaining. A highly recommended, consumable "Activity Section" provides puzzles for kids and motivates them to grab a pencil. Rounding out this truly exceptional book is a simple glossary to help expand the vocabularies of inquisitive young minds.

Francie Hill, from the *Ringling Eagle* paper, writes:

> This book would be a wonderful resource for teachers to use for a study of marine life and its animal inhabitants. While written primarily for children, much of the text would be "over the heads" of young children. An adult would need to read and interpret technical data and put the story into simpler language. People of all ages would enjoy the gorgeous illustrations and the antics of the little sea otters. Definitely those reading this book would learn a lot of information about animals and plants that live in our oceans. There is a glossary explaining unfamiliar words; also, there's an activity section with puzzles, memory quizzes and animal and plant classification.

> You can order these books at:

➢ www.gsharpproductions.com
➢ Any bookstore
➢ Amazon.com

Index

About The Author

George Kingston is a graduate of California State University, Chico, with a degree in biology. He also received an MBA from San Francisco State University. In addition to being an accomplished author, George serves as a certified financial planner and financial advisor. Success as a financial advisor and family support from his wife, Gail, have allowed him to write books. George continues to live and work in Los Gatos, California, approximately 60 miles from San Francisco. His first book, Goldilocks Makes Friends, began his personal adventure as a storyteller for children across the globe. His second book, The Exciting Adventure of Hydra and Muste Otter, allows one to learn about life in the sea through the lives of two otters, which interact with other creatures of the sea.